这一天终于来临，我们毕业了。我们即将踏上各自的征程，开始新的冒险。要记得，和心中的信念相比，逝去的遗憾和未知的艰难都微不足道。

The day has finally arrived—it's our graduation time. We are about to travel different roads, heading for new adventure. Just remember, what lies behind us and what lies before us are tiny matters compared to what lies within us.

那一年，我们一起毕业

徐玲燕／编译

江苏人民出版社

图书在版编目（CIP）数据

那一年，我们一起毕业：英汉对照 / 徐玲燕编译． --
南京：江苏人民出版社，2016.1
ISBN 978-7-214-17085-9

Ⅰ．①那… Ⅱ．①徐… Ⅲ．①英语—汉语—对照读物 Ⅳ．① H319.4

中国版本图书馆 CIP 数据核字（2015）第 311089 号

书　　名　那一年，我们一起毕业：英汉对照
编 译 者　徐玲燕
责任编辑　朱　超
装帧设计　浪殿设计　飞　扬
版式设计　张文艺
出版发行　凤凰出版传媒股份有限公司
　　　　　江苏人民出版社
出版社地址　南京市湖南路1号A楼，邮编：210009
出版社网址　http://www.jspph.com
　　　　　http://jsrmcbs.tmall.com
经　　销　凤凰出版传媒股份有限公司
印　　刷　北京中印联印务有限公司
开　　本　718 毫米 ×1000 毫米 1/16
印　　张　12
字　　数　147 千字
版　　次　2016 年 5 月第 1 版　2016 年 5 月第 1 次印刷
标准书号　978-7-214-17085-9
定　　价　24.00元

Gone Are the Days Upon Graduation

那一年，我们一起毕业

Graduation: Letting Go, Moving on
正当毕业时：放手过去，放眼未来

◎ Wendy Strgar

There is a good reason they call these ceremonies "commencement exercises". Graduation is not the end, it's the beginning.

——Orrin Hatch

I attended my son's high school graduation tonight and listened as one of his classmates shared a quote from Winston Churchill: "Success is not final, failure is not fatal: it is the courage to continue that counts." The young man recounted his own experience of multiple college rejections and concluded that trying and failing is always better than not trying at all. His wisdom about the effort and courage to continue despite the odds gave the ceremony the meaning I was searching for.

Graduations have been an ambivalent experience for me since my own. Clouded by an old narrative of my dysfunctional original family, I had never really felt like the graduation was a commencement for me. I was not able to begin from this point, as I think many people, both kids and families, struggle with the letting go and moving forward that these moments bring up.

在英文里，毕业典礼的字面义可以是“开始的仪式”，这正恰如其分地说明了，毕业不是一种结束，而是新的起始。

——奥林·哈奇

今晚，我参加了儿子的高中毕业典礼，典礼上他的一位同学分享了温斯顿·丘吉尔的一句名言：“成功无止境，失败无绝境；然勇气长存。”小伙子接着讲述了自己申请大学却一再被拒的经历，并总结道，无果的放手一搏总好过畏缩不前。即使希望渺茫，也要通过努力藉以勇气继续前行，这样的智慧让我感受到了这个典礼的意义所在。

自从我自己的毕业典礼以来，毕业时分就成为我的一种情绪复杂的体验。长期笼罩在先前父母关系失和的阴影里，我没法觉得毕业可以让我重新开始。我无法站在这样的起点上前进，就像在我看来，对许多孩子和他们的家庭来说，这一刻带给他们的只是对过往的纠结和对未来的茫然。

放手过去，不论外在看起来是否真的已然豁达，这一过程都应当始于内心。那些在心底尚未尘埃落定的事会如影随形。所以，只有当我们正视

Letting go is a process that starts on the inside if it has any chance of success on the outside. What is unresolved in us stays with us. New beginnings happen in us naturally when the past is acknowledged and assimilated into our present. Pearl Buck wrote: "Growth itself contains the germ of happiness." The urge to grow and move forward is as natural to the human species as our need to sleep, eat and love. We are born for the continuous change and development that our life time permits.

This process of moving forward is more easily accomplished as we master the letting go. Sometimes all it takes is having the courage to shine the light of our attention on the places inside of us that need to be heard. It is actually remarkable how quickly wounds that have stayed with us for decades, emotional imprints that seemed intractable will lift and shift with this simple decision to pay attention to ourselves.

I am grateful to have witnessed this process of letting go and moving forward for so many young people who I still fondly remember as small children. Watching all the caps fly, I too got the lift. We can graduate in ourselves anytime we are ready. The commencement exercise is always there for all of us.

过去，接纳过去，新的开端才会在当下自然而然地发生。赛珍珠曾写道，“成长本身就滋生孕育着幸福。”于人类来说，对成长和前进的渴求就像吃饭、睡觉、恋爱一样自然。我们生而就要在有限的生命里不断改变和进步。

如果能够放手过去，那么着眼未来就再容易不过了。有时候做到这一点，只需要我们拿出勇气，多倾听自己心灵深处的声音。只是简单地观照一下自己的内心，结果却可能超乎想象，那些已经相伴数十年的创伤，或者那些看起来无法愈合的情感伤痕，都将从心上迅速地移除转化。

我心怀感激，为能够见证许多年轻人经历这样的过程，他们放下过去，征逐未来，虽然在记忆中我还愿意当他们是小孩子。礼帽腾空的瞬间，我的精神也随之得到升华。其实只要做好了准备，人生中我们随时都可以为自己结业，而毕业典礼永远在那里等着我们。

目 录 | CONTENTS

感恩的心 · 有爱相伴

跫音回响 · 心曲哲思

搏击未来·追梦之路

采撷风致 · 趣事漫谈

感恩的心 · 有爱相伴

Some people come into our lives and quickly go. Some stay for a while and leave footprints on our hearts. And we are never, ever the same.

有些人在我们的生命中匆匆走过，有些人短暂停留却成为一生的记忆。而我们，已然因之改变。

Mr. Washington
华盛顿先生

◎ Les Brown

One day in 11th grade, I went into a classroom to wait for a friend of mine. When I went into the room, the teacher, Mr. Washington, suddenly appeared and asked me to go to the board to write something, to work something out. I told him that I couldn't do it. And he said, "Why not?"

I said, "Because I'm not one of your students."

He said, "It doesn't matter. Go to the board anyhow."

I said, "I can't do that."

He said, "Why not?"

And I paused because I was somewhat embarrassed. I said, "Because I'm Educable Mentally Retarded."

He came from behind his desk and he looked at me and he said, "Don't ever say that again. Someone's opinion of you does not have to become your reality."

It was a very liberating moment for me. On one hand, I was humiliated because the other students laughed at me. They knew that I was in Special Education. But on the other hand, I was liberated because he began to bring to my attention that I did not have to live within the context of what another person's view of me was.

美丽校训励我心

Oxford University: The Lord is my illumination.

牛津大学：上帝照亮吾之蒙昧。

读十一年级的一天，我到一间教室去等我的一个朋友。正当我走进教室时，讲台上的老师，华盛顿先生，忽然注意到了我，并叫我到黑板上解一些题目。我告诉他，我不能。他问："为什么？"

"因为我不是您的学生。"

"那没关系，到黑板前来吧。"

我仍然说："我不能。"

他又问："为什么？"

我窘迫地迟疑了一下，然后回答："我是一名可教型智力迟钝儿童。"

他从讲台后抽身到我近前，注视着我："别再这么说自己了。那只是别人对你的看法，那不一定就是你。"

那一刻我如梦方醒。一方面，其他学生知道了我在接受特殊教育的事实，他们的嘲笑使我当众出丑；但另一方面，我却释怀了，因为他让我开始懂得，我不必活在他人的眼光中。

就这样，华盛顿先生成了我生活中的良师。在此之前，我已有过两次失败的经历。一次是在五年级时被鉴定为智力迟钝，并因此降级到了四年级；到了八年级，我又遭遇了一次降级。眼前的这个人却让我的人生彻底转变了。

And so Mr. Washington became my **mentor**[①]. Prior to this experience, I had failed twice in school. I was identified as Educable Mentally Retarded in the fifth grade, put back from the fifth grade into the fourth grade, and failed again, when I was in the eighth grade. So this person made a dramatic difference in my life.

I always say that he operates in the consciousness of Goethe, who said, "Look at a man the way that he is, he only becomes worse. But look at him as if he were what he could be, and then he becomes what he should be."

Like Calvin Lloyd, Mr. Washington believed that "Nobody rises to low expectations." This man always gave students the feeling that he had high expectations for them and we **strove**[②], all of the students strove, to live up to what those expectations were.

One day, when I was still a junior, I heard him giving a speech to some graduating seniors. He said to them, "You have greatness within you. You have something special. If just one of you can get a glimpse of a larger vision of yourself, of who you really are, of what it is you bring to the planet, of your specialness, then in a historical context, the world will never be the same again. You can make your parents proud. You can make your school proud. You can make your community proud. You can touch millions of people's lives." He was talking to the seniors, but it seemed like that speech was for me.

I remember when they gave him a standing **ovation**[③]. Afterwards, I caught up to him in the parking lot and I said, "Mr. Washington, do you remember me? I was in the auditorium when you were talking to the seniors."

---

① mentor ['mɛn,tɔr] n. 指导者，贤明的顾问

② strive [straɪv] v. 努力奋斗，力争

③ ovation [o'veʃən] n. 热烈鼓掌，欢呼

我一直认为他受歌德影响颇深，正如歌德曾说过："看一个人要是囿于他的现在，那么他只能倒退；若能瞻前地看他的潜质，那么他一定不会令你失望。"

和卡尔文·洛伊德一样，华盛顿先生认为："强者是需要激励的。"他总让学生们感到，他对他们有着很高的期许，于是我们向着这个期许努力，所有的学生都在为之努力，以证明我们能行。

还在读高三的一天，我听到他给一群即将毕业的学生做演讲。他慷慨陈词："你们每个人都有可取之处，也都有特别之处。倘若你们中的哪一位能跳脱局限高视自我，想想你们真正能成为什么样的人，想想你们能给这个世界带来什么，想想你们是多么的独一无二，那么，纵观历史，世界将因你们而不同！你们将让父母引以为傲，让母校引以为傲，让周遭人引以为傲，你们将牵动无数人的生活！"虽然他的这番话是说给毕业班的学生，但在我听来，却像是说给我自己的。

我记得学生们那时都站起来为他喝彩。随后，我在停车场追上了他："华盛顿先生，您还记得我吗？我刚才在礼堂听了您为毕业班做的演讲。"

"你怎么会在那儿？你还是高三生。"他说道。

"是啊，但我听出那是你在演讲，礼堂外传来你的声音，那番话就像是对我说的，先生。你说他们都有可取之处，那么，先生请告诉我，同样置身礼堂的我是不是也有可取之处呢？"我说。

他肯定地回答："没错，布朗。"

"可事实上，我的英语、数学和历史三科都没及格，为此我还要上暑期

He said, “What were you doing there? You are a junior.”

I said, “I know. But that’s a speech you were giving. I heard your voice coming through the auditorium doors. That speech was for me, Sir. You said they had greatness within them. I was in that auditorium. Is there greatness within me, Sir?”

He said, “Yes, Mr. Brown.”

“But the fact is that I failed English and math and history, and I’m going to have to go to summer school. What about that, Sir? I’m slower than most kids. I’m not as smart as my brother or my sister who’s going to the University of Miami.”

“It doesn’t matter. It just means that you have to work harder. Your grades don’t determine who you are or what you can produce in your life.”

“I want to buy my mother a home.”

“It’s possible, Mr. Brown. You can do that.” And he turned to walk away again.

“Mr. Washington?”

“What do you want now?”

“Uh, I’m the one, Sir. You remember me, remember my name. One day you’re gonna hear it. I’m gonna make you proud. I’m the one, Sir.”

School was a real struggle for me. I was passed from one grade to another because I was not a bad kid. I was a nice kid; I was a fun kid. I made people laugh. I was polite. I was respectful. So teachers would pass me on, which was not helpful to me. But Mr. Washington made demands on me. He made me **accountable**[①]. But he enabled me to believe that I could handle it, that I could do it.

He became my instructor in my senior year, even though I was in Special

① accountable [ə'kaʊntəbəl] adj. 负有责任的

补习班，这又怎能说得过去？我比大多数孩子反应迟钝，我也没哥哥姐姐聪明，考不上迈阿密大学。”

“不要紧，这些只说明你还要更加努力。你的考试成绩并不能决定你将成为什么样的人，或者你能创造怎样的人生。”

“我想给妈妈购置一个家。”

“这当然可能，布朗。你能做得到。”他转身再度要走。

“华盛顿先生？”我叫住他。

“还有什么想说？”

“呃，我会成为那个人的，先生。请记住我，记住我的名字。会有那么一天，我的名字将家喻户晓。我会让您为我自豪的。我就是那个人，先生。”

在学校里，我的日子并不好过。我之所以能够升到高一年级，完全仰仗我不是个坏学生。我品行良好，还挺有趣，能制造笑料。我很有礼貌，言行得体。所以，老师们对我只是随手放行，于我却没有任何益处。而华盛顿先生不同，他对我要求苛刻，在他那里我不再无关紧要。他让我相信自己能够担当，能够做好。

高四那年，他成为我的指导老师，即便当时我还在接受特殊教育。正常来讲，像我这样的学生不需要修学演讲和戏剧课程，但校方还是为我能上他的课创造了条件。因为我的学业表现越来越好，校长也意识到在我和华盛顿先生之间连结着一条纽带，而他对我的影响显而易见。生平第一次，我的名字出现在了光荣榜上。我多想踏上我的戏剧之旅，而只有登上光荣

Education. Normally, Special Ed students don't take Speech and Drama, but they made special provisions for me to be with him. The principal realized the kind of bonding that had taken place and the impact that he'd made on me because I had begun to do well academically. For the first time in my life I was on the honor roll. I wanted to travel on a trip with the drama and I had to be on the honor roll in order to make the trip out of town. That was a miracle for me!

Mr. Washington restructured my own picture of who I am. He gave me a larger vision of myself, beyond my mental conditioning and my circumstances.

Years later, I produced five specials that appeared on public television. I had some friends call him when my program, "You Deserve", was on the educational television channel in Miami. I was sitting by the phone waiting when he called me in Detroit. He said, "May I speak to Mr. Brown, please?"

"Who's calling?"

"You know who's calling."

"Oh, Mr. Washington, it's you."

"You were the one, weren't you?"

"Yes, Sir, I was."

榜我才有可能真正上路。奇迹眷顾我了！

华盛顿先生重塑了我的整个人生轨迹，他没有让我因为智力状况和自身处境而看轻自己，他让我超越了自身局限。

多年以后，我制作的五辑电视特别节目已经走进了千家万户。当片子《归功于你》在迈阿密教育频道播出时，我通过朋友联系到了华盛顿先生。当他从底特律打来电话时，我就等在话机旁。“布朗先生在吗？”

“哪一位？”

“你一定知道我是谁。”

“是你，华盛顿先生。”

“你已经成为那个人了，是吗？”

“嗯，我做到了，先生。”

A Gift From God
上帝的礼物

© John W. Schlatter

One day, when I was a freshman in high school, I saw a kid from my class was walking home from school. His name was Kyle. It looked like he was carrying all of his books. I thought to myself, "Why would anyone bring home all his books on a Friday? He must really be a **nerd**①."

I had quite a weekend planned (parties and a football game with my friends tomorrow afternoon), so I shrugged my shoulders and went on.

As I was walking, I saw a bunch of kids running toward him. They ran at him, knocking all his books out of his arms and tripping him so he landed in the dirt. His glasses went flying, and I saw them land in the grass about ten feet from him. He looked up and I saw this terrible sadness in his eyes. My heart went out to him. So, I jogged over to him as he **crawled**② around looking for his glasses, and I saw tears in his eyes.

As I handed him his glasses, I said, "Those guys are jerks. They really should get lives."

He looked at me and said, "Hey thanks!" There was a big smile on his face.

---

① nerd [nɚd] n. 书呆子；讨厌鬼

② crawl [krɔl] v. 爬行，匍匐前进

美丽校训励我心

Cambridge University: From here, light and sacred draughts.

剑桥大学：启蒙之光，智慧之源，求出于此。

当我还是高一新生时，有一天，我看见班上的一位同学正走在回家的路上。他叫凯尔。他好像要把自己所有的书都往家里搬，我暗自想，到周五了，怎么会有人把全部的书都带回家呢？一定是个书呆子。

我的周末早就安排得满满的了——派对之余，还要在周六下午和朋友们打橄榄球。我耸耸肩，继续走我的路。

我正走着，迎面看到一群孩子朝他奔去。他们冲向他，撞翻他怀里的书，还将他绊倒在泥地里。他的眼镜顺势飞了出去，眼见着落在了十英尺外的草丛里。他抬起头，我看到那眼神中的痛楚。我的心也替他难过，于是我小跑到他跟前。他正趴在地上四处找他的眼镜，我看到他的眼中有泪花。

我把眼镜递给他，安慰他说，“一帮小混混，他们真该找点正经事做。”

他看着我，“嘿，谢谢你！”他的脸上展现出灿烂的笑容。这笑容里流露出发自内心的感激之情。

我帮忙拾起他的书，询问了他的住处，没想到我们竟住得很近。我很

It was one of those smiles that showed real gratitude.

I helped him pick up his books, and asked him where he lived. As it turned out, he lived near me, so I asked him why I had never seen him before. He said he had gone to private school before now. I would have never hung out with a private school kid before.

We talked all the way home, and I carried his books. He turned out to be a pretty cool kid. I asked him if he wanted to play football on Saturday with me and my friends. He said yes.

We hung all weekend and the more I got to know Kyle, the more I liked him. And my friends thought the same of him. Monday morning came, and there was Kyle with the huge stack of books again. I stopped him and said, "Darn boy, you are gonna really build some serious muscles with this pile of books everyday!" He just laughed and handed me half the books.

Over the next four years, Kyle and I became best friends. When we were seniors, we began to think about college. Kyle decided on Georgetown, and I was going to Duke. I knew that we would always be friends, that the miles would never be a problem. He was going to be a doctor, and I was going for business on a football scholarship.

Kyle was **valedictorian**① of our class. I teased him all the time about being a nerd. He had to prepare a speech for graduation. I was so glad it wasn't me having to get up there and speak.

Graduation day, I saw Kyle. He looked great. He was one of those guys that really found himself during high school. He filled out and actually looked good in glasses. He had more dates than me and all the girls loved him!

Boy, sometimes I was jealous. Today was one of those days. I could see that

① valedictorian [ˌvælɪdɪk'tɔriən] n. 致告别辞的毕业生代表

诧异，为什么从没见过他？他说，在这之前他一直在念私立学校。要是换做以前，我根本不会想和一个私校生走在一起。

我帮他拿书，之后便一路聊到家。我发现他很有趣，就问他愿不愿意周六跟我和朋友们打球，他答应了。

整个周末我们都呆在一起，愈了解凯尔，我愈觉得喜欢他。我的朋友们也都觉得他不错。到了周一早晨，凯尔和他的一大摞书又一起出现了。我招呼他，“死小子，天天拿着这堆书，你是想练成大块头吗？”他被我逗乐了，把书分了一半给我。

接下来的四年里，凯尔和我成了要好的朋友。临毕业那年，我们要报考大学了。凯尔决定去念乔治城大学，而我则选择去往杜克大学。我知道我们会是一辈子的朋友，哪怕远隔千里。他立志学医，而我准备拿到橄榄球奖学金后攻读商务专业。

凯尔是优秀毕业生，将代表我们班致告别辞。我总笑他是个书呆子。他得为毕业典礼的演讲做准备，我倒很庆幸站在大家面前发言的不是我。

毕业那天，我见到凯尔，他看起来棒极了。他是那种在高中时代真正明了自我的人。他还长胖了点，眼镜很衬托他的气质。他的约会比我要多，是女孩们竞相追逐的对象呢！

我得说，有时我真羡慕他，譬如像今天这样的时刻。我看到演讲前他有些紧张，就用力地拍了下他的后背，鼓励他说，“嘿，好小子，你很了不起。”他望着我，笑容里又是那般神情，有种发自内心的感激。“谢谢，”他说。

he was nervous about his speech. So, I **smacked**[1] him on the back and said, "Hey, big guy, you'll be great!" He looked at me with one of those looks (the really grateful one) and smiled. "Thanks," he said.

As he started his speech, he cleared his throat, and began. "Graduation is a time to thank those who helped you make it through those tough years. Your parents, your teachers, your siblings, maybe a coach…but mostly, your friends. I am here to tell all of you that being a friend to someone is the best gift you can give him. I am going to tell you a story."

I just looked at my friend with disbelief as he told the story of the first day we met. He had planned to kill himself over the weekend. He talked of how he had cleaned out his **locker**[2] so his mom wouldn't have to do it later and was carrying his stuff home. He looked hard at me and gave me a little smile. "Thankfully, I was saved. My friend saved me from doing the unspeakable."

I heard the gasp go through the crowd as this handsome, popular boy told us all about his weakest moment. I saw his mom and dad looking at me and smiling that same grateful smile. Not until that moment did I realize its depth.

Never underestimate the power of your actions. With one small gesture you can change a person's life. For better or for worse. God puts us all in each other's lives to impact one another in some way. Look for God in others.

Each day is a gift from God! Don't forget to say, "Thank you!"

① smack [smæk] v. 拍，打，掴
② locker [ˈlɑkɚ] n. 寄物柜

演讲开始之际，他先清了清嗓子，然后便开始了，“毕业之时，我们总要感激那些曾帮助我们渡过难关的人。父母，老师，兄弟姐妹，或某一位教练……但最该感谢的，恐怕是你的朋友们。在这儿我要对你们说，成为某个人的朋友就是你能给他的最好礼物。我想给你们讲一个故事。”

当他讲起我们第一次见面的情景时，我难以置信地看着我的这位朋友。原来那个周末他是打算自杀的。他说到他如何清理好了自己柜子里的所有物品，想全部带回家，这样日后就不必烦劳他妈妈了。他特意看向我，微微一笑，“谢天谢地，我被救了下来。是我的朋友阻止了我做这等傻事。”

当眼前这位英俊潇洒、颇受欢迎的小伙子吐露自己曾经的软弱时，我听到人群中发出一片感慨。而他的爸妈也在看向我，同样对我报以感激的微笑。直到此刻，我才明白这份感激的深意。

永远不要低估自身行为的力量。哪怕一个小小的举动，也可能改变他人的生活，不论这个影响是好是坏。上帝安排我们出现在他人的生命中，就是希望我们彼此间能够相互影响。那么，就请在他人身上寻求上帝的旨意吧。

每一天都是上帝赐予我们的礼物。别忘了对他人说，“谢谢你！”

The List

一份名单

◎ Helen P. Mrosla

He was in the first third grade class I taught at Saint Mary's School in Morris, Minn. All 34 of my students were dear to me, but Mark Eklund was one in a million. Very neat in appearance, but had that happy-to-be-alive attitude that made even his occasional **mischievousness**① delightful.

Mark talked incessantly. I had to remind him again and again that talking without permission was not acceptable. What impressed me so much, though, was his sincere response every time I had to correct him for misbehaving—"Thank you for correcting me, Sister!"

I didn't know what to make of it at first, but before long I became accustomed to hearing it many times a day.

One morning my patience was growing thin when Mark talked once too often, and then I made a **novice**② teacher's mistake. I looked at Mark and said, "If you say one more word, I am going to tape your mouth shut!"

It wasn't ten seconds later when Chuck blurted out, "Mark is talking again." I hadn't asked any of the students to help me watch Mark, but since I had stated

① mischievousness ['mɪstʃəvəs,nɪs] n. 恶作剧，调皮

② novice ['nɑvɪs] n. 初学者，新手

美丽校训励我心

Yale University: Truth and light.

耶鲁大学：真理与光明。

我在位于明尼苏达州莫里斯的圣玛丽学校教书时，他是我教的第一个三年级班上的学生。全班34个学生个个都是我的宝贝，但马克·艾科龙却是他们中的活宝。他穿戴整洁，老是一脸无忧无虑的样儿，以至于偶尔的小促狭都那么讨喜。

马克总爱说个不停，为此我不得不一再地提醒他，未经允许就随便讲话是不对的。每当我这样纠正他的行为时，他诚恳的回应总能打动我，“谢谢你的指正，修女！”

起初我还有点无所适从，但没过多久，我就开始习惯每天听上这句好多遍了。

一天早上，马克又在讲个不停。不耐烦之下，我犯了个初为人师才会露出的错误。我盯着马克说：“再敢说一个字，我就把你的嘴巴封上！”

没出十秒钟，另一个学生乔可就嚷道：“马克又在讲话了。”我并没有让学生们监督马克的意思，但既然我已经把丑话说在全班面前，我就得说话算数。接下来的一幕我记忆犹新，就像今早才刚发生过一样。我走到讲

the punishment in front of the class, I had to act on it. I remember the scene as if it had occurred this morning. I walked to my desk, very deliberately opened my drawer and took out a roll of masking tape. Without saying a word, I proceeded to Mark's desk, tore off two pieces of tape and made a big X with them over his mouth. I then returned to the front of the room.

As I glanced at Mark to see how he was doing, he winked at me. That did it! I started laughing. The class cheered as I walked back to Mark's desk, removed the tape, and shrugged my shoulders. His first words were, "Thank you for correcting me, Sister."

At the end of the year, I was asked to teach junior-high math. The years flew by, and before I knew it Mark was in my classroom again. He was more handsome than ever and just as polite. Since he had to listen carefully to my instruction in the "new math", he did not talk as much in ninth grade as he had in third.

One Friday, things just didn't feel right. We had worked hard on a new concept all week, and I sensed that the students were frowning, frustrated with themselves and edgy with one another. I had to stop this **crankiness**[①] before it got out of hand. So I asked them to list the names of the other students in the room on two sheets of paper, leaving a space between each name. Then I told them to think of the nicest thing they could say about each of their classmates and write it down. It took the remainder of the class period to finish their assignment, and as the students left the room, each one handed me the papers. Charlie smiled. Mark said, "Thank you for teaching me, Sister. Have a good weekend."

That Saturday, I wrote down the name of each student on a separate sheet of paper, and I listed what everyone else had said about that individual. On Monday

① crankiness ['kræŋki,nɪs] n. 坏脾气；暴躁；古怪

桌旁，慢吞吞地拉开抽屉，拿出一卷胶布。之后我一言不发地走到马克桌前，撕下来两截，在他嘴上贴了个大大的X，便回到教室前面。

我瞥了一眼马克，想看他作何反应，谁料他却朝我眨巴眨巴眼睛。他又来这套！我忍不住笑了出来。在全班的大呼小叫声中，我走回马克桌前，揭下胶布，无奈地耸耸肩。他开口的第一句话便是："谢谢你的指正，修女！"

那一年末，我被调去初中班教数学。时光荏苒，恍然间马克就又来到了我的班上。他比以前更加帅气了，却还是那么彬彬有礼。也许是因为他必须认真听我讲解"新数学"，九年级的他已不像三年级时那么爱讲话了。

那个周五，大家的情绪有点不对头。我们花了一整周时间学习一个新概念，却效果不佳，我注意到孩子们都皱着眉头，他们对自己感到泄气，又相互迁怒。我得在一切失控前赶紧缓解这种焦躁的气氛。于是，我让大家拿出两张纸，把班上除自己之外其他同学的名字写在上面，名字间留出空白。然后我让他们想一想每位同学最优秀之处，并把赞美之词一一写下来。大家用那堂课剩余的时间完成了这项任务，下课离开教室时，他们各自把纸张交了上来。查理微笑着。马克则对我说："谢谢你的教导，修女！周末愉快！"

周六，我把每个人的名字单独列在一张纸上，然后写下其他人对他的评价。到了周一，我把写好的名单发到每个人手里。不一会儿，全班同学的脸上就都扬起了微笑。

I gave each student his or her list. Before long, the entire class was smiling.

"Really?" I heard whispered. "I never knew that meant anything to anyone!"

"I didn't know others liked me so much."

No one ever mentioned those papers in class again. I never knew if they discussed them after class or with their parents, but it didn't matter. The exercise had accomplished its purpose. The students were happy with themselves and one another again.

That group of students moved on. Several years later, after I returned from vacation, my parents met me at the airport. As we were driving home, Mother asked me the usual questions about the trip—the weather, my experiences in general.

There was a **lull**① in the conversation. Mother gave Dad a sideways glance and simply says, "Dad?" My father cleared his throat as he usually did before something important.

"The Eklunds called last night," he began.

"Really?" I said. "I haven't heard from them in years. I wonder how Mark is."

Dad responded quietly. "Mark was killed in Vietnam," he said. "The funeral is tomorrow, and his parents would like it if you could attend."

To this day I can still point to the exact spot on I-494 where Dad told me about Mark.

I had never seen a serviceman in a military coffin before. Mark looked so handsome, so mature. All I could think at that moment was, "Mark, I would give all the masking tapes in the world if only you would talk to me."

---

① lull [lʌl] n. 暂停，间歇

“真的吗？”有人轻声说，“我从没想过自己这样有意义。”

“我都不知道自己这么受欢迎。”

后来，再没有人在课堂上提起过名单的事。我也不晓得他们私下里是否与同学或者父母讨论过，不过这都不重要了。对每个人来讲，这份名单已经起到了很好的作用。同学们又重新变得自信、融洽起来。

再后来，这批学生就升学了。若干年后，有一次我度假回来，父母到机场接我。开车回家的路上，母亲照例问我旅途的事，天气怎么样，去了哪些地方，诸如此类。

有一瞬间谈话停住了。母亲斜睨了父亲一眼，简短地迸出两个字：“她爸？”父亲清了清嗓子，以往有郑重的事要说时他就会这样。

“艾科龙家昨晚来电话了。”他说。

“是吗？”我有点惊讶，“好多年没他们的消息了，真想知道马克现在怎么样。”

父亲的回答却很平静，“马克在越战中牺牲了。”然后他说，“葬礼就在明天，他父母希望你能出席。”

时至今日，我仍能忆起当初父亲告诉我马克的消息时，车子行驶在I–494州际公路上的确切位置。

这是我第一次见到军人躺在军用棺材里的样子。马克看上去是成熟又帅气。那一刻，我脑中唯一的想法就是，“马克，只要你还能和我说说话，我愿用这世上所有的胶布来换。”

教堂里挤满了马克的朋友，乔可的姐姐唱起《共和国战歌》。

The church was packed with Mark's friends. Chuck's sister sang "The Battle Hymn of the Republic".

Why did it have to rain on the day of the funeral? It was difficult enough at the graveside. The pastor said the usual prayers, and the bugler played taps. One by one those who loved Mark took a last walk by the coffin and sprinkled it with holy water. I was the last one to bless the coffin. As I stood there, one of the soldiers who acted as **pallbearer**[①] came up to me.

"Were you Mark's math teacher?" he asked. I nodded as I continued to stare at the coffin. "Mark talked about you a lot," he said.

After the funeral, most of Mark's former classmates headed to Chuck's farmhouse for lunch. Mark's mother and father were there, obviously waiting for me. "We want to show you something," his father said, taking a wallet out of his pocket.

"They found this on Mark when he was killed. We thought you might recognize it."

Opening the billfold, he carefully removed two worn pieces of notebook paper that had obviously been taped, folded and refolded many times. I knew without looking that the papers were the ones on which I had listed all the good things each of Mark's classmates had said about him.

"Thank you so much for doing that," Mark's mother said. "As you can see, Mark treasured it."

Mark's classmates started to gather around us.

Charlie smiled rather **sheepishly**[②] and said, "I still have my list. It's in the top drawer of my desk at home."

---

① pallbearer ['pɔl,bɛrɚ] n. 护柩者，棺侧送葬者

② sheepishly ['ʃipɪʃlɪ] adv. 羞怯地，窘迫地；温顺地，愚蠢地

为什么此情此景还要下雨呢？站在墓前，人心格外难受。伴随着乐手的吹奏，牧师做了例行的祝祷。在场的亲人朋友，一个接一个地，最后一次走向马克的棺木，抛洒圣水。我是最后一个祝福逝者的人。当我站在马克棺前时，刚刚护柩的一位士兵向我走来。

“您就是马克的数学老师吧？”他问。我的眼睛注视着棺木，点了点头。“马克常常提起您。”他又说。

葬礼过后，马克的老同学们大多前往乔可的农庄用午餐。马克的父母亲还站在那里，显然是为了等我。“我们想给你看样东西。”他父亲边说边从口袋里掏出一个皮夹。

“马克死时，他们在他身上找到了这个。我们想您也许认得出来。”

打开钱夹，他小心翼翼地取出两张已经破损的笔记纸，显然它们曾被折了又折，粘了又粘。不用看我就知道，一定是那份名单，那份列着同学们的赞美之词的名单。

“感谢你为他做了这些，”马克的母亲说，“你也看到了，马克一直很珍视它。”

同学们这时也围了过来。

查理腼腆地一笑，说：“我也保存着我的名单呢，就在我家书桌抽屉的最上层。”

乔可的妻子则说：“乔可让我把他的那份镶在了结婚纪念册里。”

“我的也在，”玛丽莲说，“就夹在我的日记里。”

Chuck's wife said, "Chuck asked me to put his in our wedding album."

"I have mine too," Marilyn said. "It's in my diary."

Then Vicki, another classmate, reached into her pocketbook, took out her wallet and showed her worn and frazzled list to the group.

"I carry this with me at all times," Vicki said without batting an eyelash. "I think we all saved our lists."

That's when I finally sat down and cried. I cried for Mark and for all his friends who would never see him again.

接着是维琪，又一位同学，伸手从手提包里拿出钱夹，给我们大家看了她那份残破皱折的名单。

“我一直随身带着它，”维琪极为泰然地说，“我想我们都保存了自己的那一份名单。”

此刻，我才终于坐下来哭了。我哭了，为马克，也为这班再也见不到马克的朋友们。

To Tell the Truth

选择诚实

◎ Al Batt

"Who did this?" asked my teacher. Thirty children tried to think about not only what they had done, but also what our teacher may have found out. "Who did this?" asked my teacher once more. She wasn't really asking, she was demanding an answer. She seldom became angry, but she was this time. She held up a piece of broken glass and asked, "Who broke this window?"

"Oh, oh," I thought. I was the one who broke the window. I had not done it intentionally. It was caused by an **errant**① throw of a baseball. I was working on my **knuckleball**②. It needed more work. Why did it have to be me? It wasn't really my fault. If I admitted guilt, I would be in a lot of trouble. How would I be able to pay for a big window like that? I didn't even get an allowance. "My father is going to **have a fit**③," I thought. I didn't want to raise my hand, but some force much stronger than I was pulled it skyward. I told the truth. "I did it." I said no more. It was hard enough saying what I had done.

My teacher went to one of our library shelves and took down a book. She then began walking towards my desk. I had never known my teacher to strike a

① errant ['ɛrənt] adj. 犯错误的，出格的；迷途的

② knuckleball ['nʌkəl,bɔl] n.（棒球）蝴蝶球，弹指球

③ have a fit 大发脾气；大吃一惊

美丽校训励我心

Stanford University: Let the wind of freedom blow.

斯坦福大学：让自由之风劲吹。

“谁干的？”老师问道。在场的 30 个孩子不仅开始回想自己做了什么，更想知道老师会调查出什么结果。“谁干的？”老师又问了一次。语气间已不像是在询问实情，而是在盘问逼供。她很少发火，但此刻她真的动怒了。她举着一块碎玻璃，继续厉声问道：“谁打碎了玻璃？”

“噢，天啊。”我暗自想，我就是那个打碎玻璃的人。但我并不是存心的，只怪刚才打棒球时一下扔球失了手。当时我正在练习蝴蝶球，技术还不是很熟练。可为什么倒霉的偏偏是我？怨不得我啊。如果此时站出来承认错误，我就会惹上很多麻烦。我哪有钱赔偿这么一大块玻璃的损失啊？我压根就没有零花钱。“父亲一定会大发雷霆的。”我胡乱想着。尽管我不情愿举手承认，但还是有一股比自身更强大的力量迫使我举起了手臂。我说了实话，“是我干的。”除此之外，我再说不出别的话来，我实在感到很难为情。

这时，老师走到一排书架前，取下一本书，随后向我的课桌走来。我还没听说过我的老师会体罚学生，但此刻我很担心成为她的第一个牺牲品，

student, but I feared she was going to start with me and she was going to use a book for the **swatting**[①].

"I know how you like birds," she said as she stood looking down at my guilt-ridden face. "Here is that field guide about birds that you are constantly checking out. It is yours. It's time we got a new one for the school anyway. The book is yours and you will not be punished as long as you remember that I am not rewarding you for your misdeed, I am rewarding you for your truthfulness."

I couldn't believe it! I wasn't being punished and I was getting my very own bird field guide. It was the very one that I had been saving up money to buy, which money I feared would be going to the school to buy a new window. I wore out that book trying to match the live, flying birds to their depictions in that field guide. The book is gone, so is my wonderful teacher. All that remains of that day is my memory and the lesson my teacher taught me. That lesson stays with me every day and it will echo forever.

① swat [swɑt] v. 重拍，猛击

而那本书恐怕就是体罚我的武器。

“我知道你喜欢鸟类，”她停下脚步，望着我一脸负疚的神情，“这是那本你常翻阅的关于鸟类的野外指南。现在它是你的了，反正架子上也该换本新的。不仅这本书是你的，你也不会受到任何惩罚。只是你要记得，我奖励你可不是因为你做错了事，而是因为你勇于承认。”

我简直不敢相信这一幕！我没有受到一丁点惩罚，还意外获得了我心爱的那本鸟类野外指南。要知道，为了买这本书，我正拼命攒钱，刚才还很担心这些钱也要赔给学校买一块新玻璃呢。那本书后来被我翻破了，正是参照书里的描述，我一一辨认出自然界中真实飞翔的鸟儿。如今，那本书已经不在了，一起消失的还有当年那位仁慈善良的老师，留给我的只有关于那天的美好回忆，还有这隽永的人生一课。这一幕将常留在我心间，永久回响。

纸条情

◎ Patty Hansen

When I was in the fifth grade, I fell in love—real love—for the very first time. It only took about a week into the school year for it to happen, and I was completely, head-over-heels crushing on Mike Daniels. No one ever called him just Mike; it was always one word—Mike Daniels. Blond hair that stuck up in every direction and blue eyes that crinkled in the corners when he laughed—visions of Mike Daniels occupied my every dream.

To say I wasn't the most popular or prettiest girl in our class would be an understatement. In fact, I think I must have been the original **geek**[1]. I was so skinny that I still had to wear days-of-the-week panties and dorky undershirts when most of my friends were starting to wear bras and more grown-up undergarments. My mom made me wear brown **orthopedic**[2] lace-up shoes to school every day, because I had a foot that turned in and my parents wanted to "correct it before it was too late". Right smack dab in the middle of my two front teeth was this giant space that even gum surgery the year before hadn't fixed, and the two teeth on either side of my front teeth overlapped, making me look

① geek [gik] n. 怪人；极客

② orthopedic [ɔrθə'pidɪk] adj. 整形的，矫正的

美丽校训励我心

Massachusetts Institute of Technology (MIT): Mind and hand.

麻省理工学院：理论与实践并重。

念五年级的时候，我第一次坠入爱河，我真正感到心动了。学期开始才一周，我就发现自己无可救药地迷恋上了麦克・丹尼尔。还没有人能只叫他麦克，通常都是麦克・丹尼尔这么连名带姓的称呼。他那金色的发丝根根张扬着，碧蓝的眼睛一笑间就在眼角漾出笑意，麦克・丹尼尔的神情举止令我魂牵梦萦。

说婉转些，我算不上班里最出众或者最漂亮的女生。照直说来，我觉得自己就是个少见的怪胎。我很瘦削，还在穿小女生的那种“一周七天”套装内裤和老土的贴身背心，而同年龄的女友们都开始穿文胸和成人内衣了。妈妈还让我每天上学都穿那双棕色系带的矫正鞋，因为我的一只脚走路有些内倾，所以爸妈想及早帮我纠正过来。而我的牙就更糟了，正中的两颗门牙间不偏不倚地留下了巨大的齿缝，一年前为此专门做了牙科整形也无济于事。更要命的是，门牙两侧的两颗牙又重叠长在一起，让我看起来像长了犬齿。再加上厚厚的眼镜片，幼细稀少的头发（这可是完全遗传

like I had fangs. Add a pair of thick glasses, thin baby-fine hair (with a home permanent from my mom—help!), **knobby**① skinned-up knees and elbows—and what do you get? A kid that only a parent could love.

I wouldn't—couldn't—tell my friends that I was in love with Mike Daniels. It was my secret to write about in my journal. In my dreams, Mike Daniels would suddenly grasp what a beautiful soul was hiding inside my **gawky**② body and realize that he loved me for who I really was. I spent hours writing poetry for him and stories about him, until one day I got up the nerve to actually write to him about how I felt.

Our teacher, Miss Finkelor, was really awesome about most things, but the one thing she was majorly serious about was not writing notes to each other during class. Everyone did it anyway. Except me. My only shot at self-esteem was being teacher's pet, and I excelled at it. I loved it so much it didn't even bother me when kids teased me about being the teacher's favorite.

It was a huge decision for me to go against the one thing that Miss Finkelor detested—note passing. But I knew that there was no other way to tell Mike Daniels about how I felt—and I also knew that if I never told him, I was going to burst… or maybe even freak out. I vowed to do it on Monday morning.

So, first thing Monday morning, in my very best printing, I wrote, "I love you". That was it. Nothing else—no flowers, no poetry—just, "I love you". I passed it to Dianne, who sat between me and Mike Daniels, and whispered, "Give this to Mike Daniels," trying to look really casual, like it was a request to borrow a book from him or something. I held my breath as I watched him open and read it—then read it again. Then he folded it up and put it into his pocket. Oh my God,

---

① knobby ['nɒbi] adj. 多节的，多突起的；棘手的

② gawky ['gɔki] adj. 迟钝的，笨拙的

自我母亲那一系——救命哦！)，瘦骨嶙峋的膝部和肘部——所有这些集于一身，你会作何感想？恐怕你也会觉得，我只有父母宠爱的份罢了。

我不愿，更不能告诉我的朋友们，说我喜欢上了麦克·丹尼尔。这只能是我在日记中独享的秘密。我幻想着，麦克·丹尼尔能蓦然发掘我笨拙外表下的美丽灵魂，意识到他因爱我的灵魂而爱上我整个人。我会用几个小时的时间为他写诗创作故事，直到某天我鼓起勇气要把我对他的感受让他知道。

我们的老师，芬科勒小姐历来很威严，对于课堂上传纸条的现象更是明令禁止。但大家都干过这件事，只有我没干过。当老师的宠儿能让我的自尊心获得无上满足，何况我轻易就能成为讨老师喜欢的那种学生。这个宠儿我当得心甘情愿，哪怕被同学们嘲笑为老师的乖乖女也不以为意。

明知暗递纸条是芬科勒小姐反感的事，我还是下了很大决心拿定这个主意。我很清楚，没有别的办法可以告诉麦克·丹尼尔我的感受；同时我也清楚，如果再不告诉他，我的情绪就会濒临崩溃，甚至不知会做出什么来。因此，我发誓要在周一早晨迈出这一步。

到了周一，我先一早用自己最漂亮的印刷字体写下“我爱你”。就这些，不需要别的点缀了，不要鲜花，不要诗情，就这三个字“我爱你”。我把纸条递给坐在我和麦克·丹尼尔中间的黛安娜，悄声道：“传给麦克·丹尼尔。”我努力装作没什么特别的，就是问他借本书或者什么东西。我屏住呼吸看着他展开纸条，看了一遍，紧接着又看了一遍。然后他把纸条折了

what have I done? What if he shows it to his buds at recess? They'll all laugh their heads off. I'm a fool. An idiot. Why did I tell him? I felt like I was going to throw up.

I was so involved in feeling like I was going to hurl, that I didn't even feel Dianne punching me in the arm. Then she **shoved**① a note in my hand. Slowly, I opened it. It was my own note. "Great, he thought it was so stupid that he sent it back to me," I thought. Then it dawned on me—he had written something on the back of it:

"I like you, too. I'm glad we're friends."

I didn't know whether to laugh or cry. I was so relieved that he didn't **trash**② me—that could have easily happened if Mike Daniels hadn't been a really nice guy. With that one little gesture of kindness, Mike Daniels made me feel special—and, not only that, but I felt that somehow, he had seen the real me hidden in the body of a fifth grade geek.

I kept that note for years—all the way through the eighth grade. Whenever I felt bad about myself, I would reread Mike Daniels' note and remember that act of kindness. It didn't matter to me what inspired him—if it was pity, or the recognition of things to come—that note gave me strength to go through the challenges of the tough years that followed fifth grade.

① shove [ʃʌv] v. 推，猛推，推开；乱塞
② trash [træʃ] v. 糟蹋，破坏，伤害；诋毁，戳伤

回去放进口袋里。哦，天啊，我做了什么？要是他在休息时把纸条拿给其他男生看，那可怎么办啊？那些人一定会笑掉下巴的。我真蠢，傻瓜一个。为什么要说出来呢？我感到自己几欲作呕。

这种感觉如此强烈地占据了我，以至于黛安娜用胳膊碰我时我都没有感觉到。她把一张纸条塞给我。我缓慢地展开它，是我刚才那张。“好吧，他一定是觉得荒唐透了，才把纸条还了回来。”我自忖。之后我才猛然意识到，他在纸条背面写了字。

“我也喜欢你，很高兴我们成为朋友。”

我不知该感动得哭出来还是笑出来。我如释重负，他没有以此捉弄我——如果麦克・丹尼尔不是真正善良的男孩子，那一幕可能早就发生了。只是这个微小的善举，麦克・丹尼尔给了我特殊的感受；不仅如此，我感到他多少看到了那个隐藏在怪异外表下的五年级小女孩的真实自我。

那张纸条我保存了许多年，一直到念完八年级。无论何时我对自己丧失信念，我都会重新看看麦克・丹尼尔的那张纸条，重温当初的那个善意的举动。他出于什么那样回应已经不重要了——不忍伤害我也好，坦然接受这份恋慕也罢，那张纸条赋予我的是勇气，让我能够勇于面对五年级之后的一切艰难挑战。

Reunited

重聚

◎ Ellen Cady

Old friends. They finish your sentences, they remember the cat that ran away when you were twelve, and they tell you the truth when you've had a bad haircut. But mostly, they are always there for you—whether it's in person or via late night phone calls—through good times and bad. But as the years pass, it becomes increasingly difficult to see each other, to make new memories. Fortunately, my high school girlfriends and I vowed long ago not to let this happen. We vowed to have reunions.

A few months ago, we met up for a three-day weekend in the American Southwest. We grew up together in Maine and have said for years that we should have an annual event, yet it's often postponed or canceled due to schedule conflicts. Not this year.

Four of us—two from San Francisco, one from Boston, and one from Seattle—boarded planes bound for Santa Fe, New Mexico, where one of the gang lives and works for an art gallery. Two years ago, she moved there—escaped, rather—from the film industry in New York City, where she led a life that felt too fast, too unfulfilling. The artist in her longed for vibrant landscapes and starry moonlit skies. She wanted to drive a truck on dusty roads, a trusty dog at her

美丽校训励我心

Princeton University: In the nation's service and in the service of all nations.

普林斯顿大学：效力国家，服务世界。

老朋友。他们会快嘴接完你想说的话，他们会记得你 12 岁那年走失的一只猫，他们会直言不讳你剪了个很烂的发型。最重要的是，他们会一直陪在你的左右——不论是亲自现身说法，还是一通午夜电话，他们就是那个与你一同分享美好时光，抑或度过艰难时期的人。可是，随着岁月的流逝，老朋友间已然越来越少见面，也愈来愈鲜有新的回忆留存。好在很早以前，我和高中女友们就立下誓约不让这样的情况出现，我们约定要再次相聚。

几个月前，我们利用周末，选在美国西南部小聚三天。我们从小一起在缅因州长大，这些年来一直都张罗着每年的聚会，可是常常因为彼此的时间冲突而一再延宕，终成哑果。今年，我们终于如愿以偿。

我们一行四人，其中两个来自旧金山，一个来自波士顿，还有一个来自西雅图，将一同飞往新墨西哥州的圣特菲，我们这群死党中有人在此定居，为一间画廊工作。两年前，因为觉得纽约的生活节奏太快，过得太失意，她选择搬来此地，其实更像是从之前的电影业中逃脱出来。艺术家的天性让她向往这里生机勃发的景象，爱上月下繁星点缀的夜空。她情愿在扬尘的土路上开着卡车，有只忠实的老狗在副驾的位子上，一路陪伴她。

side, riding shotgun. She got all that and found love, too. She is happy.

The rest of us—still big city folks—**converged**[①] on her like a **cyclone**[②]straight out of the pages of a girlfriend novel. Chattering and memory swapping, we were fifteen again—in a space of five minutes. Naturally, we relived some of the stories of our youth—angst and all—but we also brought much more to the gathering this time. We were new people. we were wives and girlfriends to someone back home. We were businesswomen, artists and writers. We were no longer girls, no longer post-college grads. We were women.

I shared an air mattress that night with my friend from Boston, the one who calls me, while **rubbernecking**[③] in traffic, to catch up on her cell phone, to tell me of her life and love. On the next mattress was a gal from San Francisco, she just newly single and enjoying her independence. Our host, the artist, shared her bedroom that weekend with a married **dot-commer**[④] from San Francisco. Yes, we are different, but we are also the same. The years of our youth say so.

The apartment was open and we talked late into the night, our voices carrying back and forth between the rooms as we laughed, cackling about things that would only be humorous to friends with this kind of history. The next morning, I awoke to a brilliant blue sky, beautifully contrasted by the earthy brown of the surrounding **adobe**[⑤]. It was Saturday and the art enthusiasts were out, so, with coffee in hand, I dropped off our host at work. I returned to find the others still in slumber, deep lines on their faces as evidence of a restful sleep.

We checked out town and headed to the airport to pick up the last

---

① converge [kən'vɚdʒ] v. 聚集，汇聚
② cyclone ['saɪ,klon] n. 旋风，飓风
③ rubberneck ['rʌbɚ,nɛk] v. 伸长脖子看（或听）
④ dot-commer n. 互联网从业人员
⑤ adobe [ə'dobi] n. 风干土坯；土砖建筑物

这一切如今都实现了，而且，她还收获了爱情，是个幸福的女人。

我们其余几个，都还生活在大城市里，这会儿一股旋风般汇聚到她身边，活脱猛然从女友小说的书页间跳出来。见了面就七嘴八舌、问长问短，用不到 5 分钟，我们就仿若重回 15 岁。我们自然而然地重温起年轻时的旧事，青春愁肠以及种种，但这次聚会的看头还不止这些。我们都有了全新的身份，或为人妻，或心有所属。我们更是商界女性、女艺术家、女性作家。我们不再是小女孩，也不再是刚毕业的女学生，我们已成为女人。

那一晚，我和波士顿女友睡在同一张充气床垫上。她会在翘首以待交通拥堵的间隙，不忘给我打上一通电话，告诉我她现在的生活状况和情感历程。旁边一张床垫上是旧金山女友，刚刚恢复单身，正享受一个人的独居时光。而我们的女主人，兼女艺术家，则在那个周末让出自己的卧室，和另一位在旧金山从事网络工作的已婚姐妹同住。的确，我们自身都有了变化，但有些东西却从未改变。那些青春岁月就是最好的证明。

房间是开放设计，我们集体聊到深夜，欢声笑语不时回荡整间屋子，也只有相识多年的老友走到一起，才会如此心领神会笑个没完吧。次日清晨醒来，碧空如洗，在周围土褐色房屋的映衬下，阳光格外明媚。因为这天是周六，艺术爱好者们出去活动的日子。于是，我手捧咖啡送我们的女主人出门，回来时看见其他人都还在睡梦中，脸上枕出的深痕说明她们睡得很香沉。

我们驱车出城，赶去机场接最后一个掉队的人，她正从旧金山赶来呆上一晚。“我怎么可能错过这次聚会呢，”她说，哪怕凌晨 4 点要赶往机场。当晚，我们喝着玛格丽特，吃着西南部美食，庆祝这难得的相聚。席间，

straggler[①], who came in from San Francisco for one night. " I wouldn't have missed this for anything," she said, despite her 4 a.m. trip to the airport. That night we celebrated margaritas and Southwestern are, each of us gazing over at the faces around the table as we wondered, who would have thought the bonds of childhood could last this long? Some of us have been friends since the age of five, some since age twelve and, yet, here we are approaching the age of thirty. Quite rapidly, I might add.

The weekend consisted of long talks by the pool, wonderful meals, and a hike that brought the entire group to tears. Not tears of sadness or anger, but an outpouring of emotion over the sheer wonderment that we can be this close—twelve years after graduation—with such physical distance between us. It's heartbreaking that we can't spend our days together in the same neighborhood, walking the same streets, reading the same newspaper at the same coffee shop. But that's life, grown-up life.

Most amazing is the group's adaptability to one another. The months we spend apart are non-existent. No need to get reacquainted, we jump back in the saddle and it's as comfortable as ever. Old friends—friends with an ever-present sense of support and sisterhood, friends that know each other innately—are hard to come by and yet we remain as tight today as we were years ago, giggling in the back row of Mr. McKechnie's 9th grade math class.

Life today, however, is no math class. Our world, spinning slightly off its axis, is full of doubt, full of fear. Yet it reminds me—now, more than ever—how vital it is that we stay in close touch. We may have questions about our future, but we have true faith in our past, and though this reunion of friends has come to a close, we are already drawing up plans for the next one.

① straggler ['stræglər] n. 落伍者，掉队的人

我们彼此相顾，不禁感慨万千，谁曾想童年结下的友谊可以维系这么久？我们中有人自5岁起就是朋友了，有些12岁时才相识，而如今，我们都快30岁了。不得不说，时光真快。

那个周末的活动还包括泳池旁的促膝长谈，共享美味佳肴，以及令所有人泪湿的一次远足。这不是伤心或负气的泪水，而是为冥冥中无法割舍的这份情谊不能自持。毕业已经12年了，彼此相距那么遥远，可是我们却还能如此亲密。一想到我们不能日日毗邻而居，走过同一条街，坐在同一间咖啡店里看同一份报，心就隐隐作痛。但，这就是生活，成年后面对的生活。

最让人感到奇妙的是，我们这群死党竟毫无生分，仿佛我们分开的那些日子不曾真的存在过。无须重新热络，提鞍上马做回自己，感觉起来还是那么舒服。所谓老朋友，就是那些无论过去现在都一路支持你，让你感到姐妹情深的人，亦是那些真正懂得你所思所想的人。这样的人一生当中很难知遇，而如今我们还能亲密如故，就像九年级那年我们在麦基契尼先生的数学课上坐在教室后排咯咯傻笑时那样。

然而，生活如今已不似当年的数学课那般轻松了。我们的世界稍微偏离了既定的轨迹，充斥着疑虑和恐惧。而这些恰在此刻提醒了我，让我比过去更清晰地感到，我们能保持这份亲密是多么难能可贵。也许我们的未来还会遇到问题，但是过去赋予我们真正的信念。尽管这次聚会已接近尾声，我们却开始策划下一次见面了。

Forever Friends

永远的朋友

◎ Carlo Martini

Sometimes in life
You find a special friend
Someone who changes your life
Just by being a part of it

Someone who makes you laugh
Until you can't stop
Someone who makes you believe
That there really is good in the world

Someone who convinces you
That there really is an unlocked door
Just waiting for you to open it
This is a forever friendship

When you're down
And the world seems dark and empty

有时候于生命中
你会觅得一位知己
只消偶尔出现在你的生活里
他就能改变你的人生

他会令你欢笑
开怀得忘乎所以
他会给你信念
人间自有真情在

他会说服于你
面前有扇不上锁的门扉
正等待你去开启
这就是永远的朋友

当你失落时
世界因此黯淡无光失去意义
你永远的朋友会鼓舞你

Your forever friend lifts you in spirit
And makes that dark and empty world

Suddenly seem bright and full
Your forever friend gets you through
The hard times, the sad times
And the confused times

If you turn and walk away
Your forever friend follows
If you lose your way
Your forever friend guides you

And cheers you on
Your forever friend holds your hand
And tells you that things
Will be okay

And if you find such a friend
You feel happy and complete
You have a forever friend for life
And forever has no end

于这黑暗空虚的世界中

顿时令你重归明亮充盈
你永远的朋友与你一起
度过这艰难困苦
摆脱混沌

如果你转身走开
你永远的朋友会跟随你
如果你失去方向
你永远的朋友会指引你

激励你一路向前
你永远的朋友会握着你的手
安慰你说
一切都会好好的

如果你觅得这样一位朋友
必将感到快乐知足
你的生命中从此有位永远的朋友
而永远没有尽头

跫音回响·心曲哲思

A certain amount of care or pain or trouble is necessary for every man at all times. A ship without ballast is unstable and will not go straight.

每个人都免不了随时要伴有一定的 忧虑、痛苦或烦恼，就像一艘船离了压舱物便很难行得稳走得正。

No One Will Ever Know

无人知晓

© Janet Seever

Karen, Judy and I were the last ones back in the school room after lunch. We put our metal lunch boxes on the shelf above the coat hooks, which were mostly empty. All of the other sixth graders were already outside, playing **marbles**[①] or **hop scotch**[②] or jumping rope, since it was a pleasant spring day.

"Look what I found this morning in the storage cupboard when I was getting out some art supplies for Mrs. Eiffler." With a **conspiratorial**[③] grin on her face, Karen held up a wooden box filled with short pieces of chalk in every color of the rainbow.

"Wow! What fun it would be to write on the chalkboard while everyone is outside." Judy's eyes twinkled with anticipation.

"But Mrs. Eiffler doesn't want us writing on the chalkboard," I responded, already feeling guilty, although we had not yet done a thing.

"Don't be such a 'fraidy cat', Janet. No one will ever know," said Karen, reaching into the box and drawing out a piece of chalk.

---

① marble ['mɑrbəl] n. 弹珠；弹子游戏

② hop scotch 跳房子

③ conspiratorial [kənˌspɪrəˈtɔriəl] adj. 阴谋的，阴谋家的；阴险的，鬼祟的

美丽校训励我心

University of Pennsylvania: Laws without morals are in vain.

宾夕法尼亚大学：法理不离道义。

我和凯伦、朱迪是午饭后最后回到教室的三个人。我们把金属饭盒放到衣帽钩上方的架子上时注意到，衣帽钩大多空着。此时室外春光明媚，六年级的其他学生都到外面玩弹珠，跳房子或者跳绳去了。

“快看我今天早上给埃芙雷夫人取颜料时在储存柜里发现了什么！”凯伦一脸诡秘的坏笑，展示给我们一个木头盒子，里面装满了五颜六色的粉笔头。

“哇，趁大家都在外面，我们几个偷偷在黑板上写字该多么好玩啊！”朱迪的眼睛里闪烁着期待的光芒。

“但是埃芙雷夫人不让我们在黑板上写字啊。”我有所顾虑地应着，此时还没做什么，我就先心虚了。

“别跟个胆小鬼似的，珍妮，没人会知道。”凯伦说着就把手伸进盒子里，拿出一小支粉笔来。

“就是啊，大家都在外面呢，我们很安全，没人会告我们的状。”朱迪说着已经胸有成竹地画起房子来。

"Right. Everyone is outside, so we're safe. No one will tell on us." Judy was already drawing a house with sure strokes.

I **reluctantly**[1] joined my friends in the artwork, wanting to be part of what was going on, but afraid of being caught. I knew well that we were breaking not one, but two class rules. The second rule was that no one was allowed to stay inside at noon without a written excuse from home if the weather was nice.

Trying various colors, we drew houses, trees and three-dimensional boxes. It was fun! All the time we were watching the clock, knowing that our fun would be over if anyone walked into the room.

Then Judy had an idea. "We're all right-handed. Let's see who can write their name best using their left hand."

Judy and Karen picked up their chalk and started writing. I chose a white piece from the box and wrote my name. The handwriting was a bit shaky, but no one would doubt that it said "Janet".

"I think Judy is the winner," said Karen. "Hers is the best."

"We'd better get this board cleaned off before Mrs. Eiffler comes back," said Judy, eying the clock. She picked up an eraser and began erasing our handiwork from the board.

Everything came off...but my name!

In disbelief, I looked at the chalk I held in my sweaty hand. On closer examination, it wasn't chalk at all. I had picked up a small piece of white color crayon which was mixed in with the pieces of chalk.

My stomach **churned**[2] and my knees felt weak. What would Mrs. Eiffler do to me?

---

① reluctantly [rɪ'lʌktəntlɪ] adv. 不情愿地，勉强地

② churn [tʃə:n] v. 剧烈搅动；翻腾

我不太情愿地加入了她们的涂鸦当中，只是想成为其中的一份子，心里还是很害怕被抓。我很清楚我们现在违反的不只是一条班纪，而是两条。这另一条班纪就是：如果天况良好，任何人都不准在午休时间留在室内，除非有家长的书面假条。

我们尝试了各种颜色，画出了房子、大树以及有立体感的盒子。太好玩了！我们始终盯着时间，因为一旦有人进来，我们的欢乐可就到头了。

这时朱迪又冒出个主意来，“我们一直都是用右手写字，不如我们看看谁用左手写自己的名字最好看吧。”

朱迪和凯伦拿起粉笔就开始写。我从盒子里挑了一根白色的，也写起自己的名字来。虽然笔迹歪歪扭扭，但谁都能看出来写的是“珍妮”。

“我觉得朱迪胜出，”凯伦说，“她的字最棒。”

“我们最好在埃芙雷夫人回来之前把黑板擦干净。”朱迪一边眼瞄时钟一边说。她抓起黑板擦开始擦掉我们的手迹。

所有的东西都擦掉了——只剩我的名字还在！

我难以置信地看了看握在手里的那根粉笔，手心都冒汗了。仔细这么一看才发现，它哪是粉笔啊，我竟然拿了一小支混在粉笔头里的白色蜡笔！

我的胃一阵翻腾，膝盖也发软了。埃芙雷夫人会怎么惩罚我呢？

我妈妈总说：“傻瓜的名笨蛋的脸，哪儿人多哪儿现眼。”以前还不太懂这话的意思，此刻我是彻底领会了！我就是那个傻瓜，晒在黑板上的大名就是佐证。而且，老师很快就要回来了。

“快，弄点儿湿纸巾来。”话音未落，朱迪就飞身行动起来。

尽管使劲一顿擦，我的名字还是没擦掉。

My mother had a saying: "Fools' names and fools' faces always appear in public places." I never understood fully what it meant before. Now I did! I was a fool, and there was my name in crayon to prove it. And the teacher would be returning soon.

"Quick, let's get some wet paper towels," said Judy, springing into action.

After vigorous rubbing, my name still remained.

"I think I saw a can of cleanser by the sink in the coat room," I said as I raced to find it. Precious minutes were ticking away.

We rubbed and my name came off all right, but in the process of removing it, we left an **abrasion**[①] on the chalkboard.

Listening for footsteps coming down the hall, we dried the scrubbed area as much as we could with more paper towels and fanned it with a book to remove every tell-tale trace of wetness.

We were just slipping into our desks as the bell rang and the other students began entering the room. The teacher walked in soon afterward.

Mrs. Eiffler never asked about abrasion and maybe never noticed it. But I did. Every time I walked past the marred surface of the chalkboard, I remembered. Oh, how I remembered.

The lesson I learned that day is one I never forgot, even though over forty years have passed since the event. "No one will ever know" is never true. Even if no one else found out, Jesus knew and I knew. Sometimes living with a guilty conscience is punishment enough.

---

① abrasion [ə'breʒən] n. 磨损；磨损处，擦伤处

“我记得在更衣室的水槽那儿有一罐清洁剂。”我说着就连忙奔过去找。宝贵的时间在嘀嗒嘀嗒地溜走。

我们又是一顿擦，这回名字终于擦掉了，可是在反复擦拭的过程中，我们把黑板擦坏了一小处。

此时，大厅里传来了脚步声，我们赶紧多拿些纸巾，尽量把刚刚擦湿的地方弄干，还抄起一本书，在有水迹的地方使劲扇着，试图灭掉所有罪证。

就在我们刚刚溜回座位时，铃声响了。其他同学陆续回到了教室，老师也紧随其后走了进来。

埃芙雷夫人从没问起过黑板上那块磨损的地方，也许是从来就没注意到。然而，我却总会留意。每当我经过黑板被损坏的地方时，我总能想起这件事。哦，我竟然记得这么牢!

即使是在事情已经过去四十多年后的今天，我仍无法忘记那一天给我的教训。“无人知晓”永远没法成立。即使没有其他人在场，还会有天知我知。有时候，遭受良心的谴责就是最好的惩罚了。

Warm Delights to Rekindle a Lost Friendship
用情牵故知

◎ Anonymous

December marked the end of my final semester in college. When nearing a landmark event like graduation, I think it's instinctive to take a step back and reevaluate, figure out what I have accomplished and what I want to accomplish. This was a rough one for me. Sadly I believe that college was a waste of my time; I don't think I learned much that will help me in the "real world".

In the wake of this depression, I tried to turn it into something semi-meaningful. I looked around at all the girls in my **sorority**① who go through their day-to-day lives, fulfilling obligations, complaining about petty things, and losing perspective. I knew I was like that too and wanted to change.

Marissa and Mackenzie were two of my sorority sisters who had been best friends in the previous year. Naturally they became roommates. They shared clothes, school supplies, the same circle of friends, and similar schedules. Inevitably, their parallel lives became a source of discontentedness. They got on each other's nerves over petty things. Their friendship weakened and their interactions were filled with arguments and conflicts. Worse yet, the arguments

① sorority [sə'rɔrɪti] n. 妇女联谊会，女生联谊会；诚挚的姐妹关系

美丽校训励我心

Cornell University: I would found an institution where any person can find instruction in any study.

康奈尔大学：吾始建校，为授天下人之所求识。

12 月标志着大学生活的最后一个学期即将结束了。当人生中诸如毕业这种历史性时刻即将到来时，我们都会本能地退后一步，重新审视一下自我，细数这几年里都实现了什么，还有什么想要实现。不过，这对我来说可够难的。遗憾地说，大学生活在我看来就是浪费时光，我自认没学到多少对日后进入社会有用的知识。

沮丧之余，我试图把这种情绪转化为某种有意义的东西，哪怕最终的意义不大也行。我环顾自己身边的姐妹淘，她们个个都在混日子，做一天和尚撞一天钟，一点小事就抱怨个不停，根本看不到前途。我知道我跟她们一样浑浑噩噩，因此我要作出点改变。

玛瑞莎和麦肯姬先前本是我们姐妹淘里最要好的两个人。自然而然她们成了室友，衣服换着穿，学习用品换着用，一样的朋友圈子，甚至一样的作息时间。久而久之，形同双胞胎的两个人难免渐生龃龉。只因为一点小事，两个人就彼此迁怒对方。她们的友谊岌岌可危，两个人在一起争吵

gradually turned into a passive resentment for one another.

Normally I do not make other people's relationships and friendships my business. I think it's **patronizing**① to the people involved, and it makes everyone uncomfortable and defensive. Somehow, though, I could not get them off my mind. These girls had been representative of what I thought a good friendship looked like. They were everything to each other and now they were the **antithesis**②. I thought about what I might do to help bring them back together. I remembered that the first few times I had met these girls, they were watching Grey's Anatomy in our TV room, and eating brownies together. They were those yummy brownies that you microwave and pour hot fudge on top of. Anyway, before I moved out of the sorority house, I bought two packages of "Warm Delights", and wrapped them up with a tag addressed to these two girls. I left it outside of their bedroom door, in hopes that they would find it, **reminisce**③, and enjoy the "Warm Delights" together. Even if they didn't fully rekindle their friendship, I'm hoping that it helped them remember why they became friends in the first place.

Too often we let people in our lives slip through the cracks. We don't have time to call or write. We get mad about silly things. We put rifts in our relationships by closing doors instead of trying to patch things up. At the very least, I hope that Mackenzie and Marissa went home for their holiday break remembering that they don't actually hate each other as much as they might think they do.

---

① patronizing ['petrə,naɪzɪŋ] adj. 屈尊俯就的，显出优越感的

② antithesis [æn'tɪθɪsɪs] n. 对照，对立；对立面

③ reminisce [,rɛmə'nɪs] v. 回忆，缅怀；叙旧

不断，分歧不断。更糟的是，这样的争吵也渐渐变成了一种彼此仇视的冷战。

通常我是不大愿意插手他人关系，或者介入别人的交情中去，我不想对当事人摆出一副高姿态，弄得所有人都不自在，甚至心存戒备。不知怎么，我却没法无视这两个女孩子。她们的存在像是为我勾勒出了女生情谊应有的样子。曾经她们好得就像一个人似的，可如今她们却成了死对头。我思量着做点什么才能重新拉近两个人的距离。我记得最初见到两个女孩子时，她们总在电视机房一起看那部叫做《实习医生格蕾》的美剧，嘴里还嚼着布朗尼。就是那种好味的果仁巧克力蛋糕，只消微波加热后倒上热的乳脂软糖即可食用。不管怎样，搬出女生宿舍前，我买了两袋“暖怡”布朗尼，包装好并写明了是送给这两个女孩的。我把这份礼物留在了她们的寝室门口，期待着她们能发现它，追忆起过去的时光，重又坐在一起分享“暖怡”的味道。即使她们不能一下子重归于好，至少我希望这份礼物能让她们回忆起当初是如何走在一起的。

很多时候，我们让生命中的一些人轻易地从心之罅隙溜走了。我们借口没时间而没能打上一通电话，或者写下一封信来表情达意，我们为一些傻问题而大动干戈。最终，关闭心门取代了弥合裂痕。最起码我希望，玛瑞莎和麦肯姬能在这次回家度假时想一想，她们其实并没有真的那么憎恨对方。

The Rock Parable

石子的寓言

◎ Gerald Nash

One day, an expert in time management was speaking to a group of business students and, to drive home a point, used an illustration those students will never forget.

As he stood in front of the group of high-powered overachievers he said,

"Okay, time for a quiz," and he pulled out a one-gallon, wide-mouth **mason jar**[①] and set it on the table in front of him. He also produced about a dozen fist-sized rocks and carefully placed them, one at a time, into the jar.

When the jar was filled to the top and no more rocks would fit inside, he asked, "Is this jar full?" Everyone in the class yelled, "Yes."

The time management expert replied, "Really?" He reached under the table and pulled out a bucket of gravel. He dumped some gravel in and shook the jar causing pieces of gravel to work themselves down into the spaces between the big rocks. He then asked the group once more, "Is the jar full?"

By this time the class was on to him. "Probably not," one of them answered.

"Good!" he replied. He reached under the table and brought out a bucket of sand. He started dumping the sand in the jar and it went into all of the spaces left

---

① mason jar 梅森食品瓶（一种有密封螺旋盖的家用大口玻璃瓶）

美丽校训励我心

Washington University: Strength through Truth.

华盛顿大学：真理彰显力量。

一天，时间管理专家给一班商学专业的学生授课。课堂上，为了把观点阐释清楚，他援用了一个实例，其中的寓意令学生们永远难忘。

站在这群风头正健、出类拔萃的学生面前，他说：

“下面，我们来做个测试。”说着便拿出一个容积 1 加仑的广口梅森瓶，放在他面前的桌子上。接着，他又拿出十来个拳头大小的石块，小心翼翼地把它们一块一块放进瓶子里。

等石块装满瓶口，再也装不下时，他问：“瓶子满了吗？”人家高声回答：“满了。”

这时，时间管理专家回应道：“真的满了吗？”只见他从桌子下面提上来一桶碎石子，把其中一些倒进瓶子里，摇晃瓶身以便这些碎石能够填充到石块间的空隙中去。然后，他又问同学们：“这次瓶子满了吗？”

此时大家有点心领神会了。“可能还没满吧。”一个学生答道。

“好！”说完他又伸手从桌子下面拎出一桶细沙，开始把细沙往瓶子里倒，沙子很快填满了石块与碎石间留下的所有缝隙，他再一次问道：“瓶子满了吗？”“没满！”全班都大声回答。

between the rocks and the gravel. Once more he asked the question, "Is this jar full?" "No!" the class shouted.

Once again he said, "Good." Then he grabbed a **pitcher**① of water and began to pour it in until the jar was filled to the **brim**②. Then he looked at the class and asked, "What is the point of this illustration?"

One **eager beaver**③ raised his hand and said, "The point is, no matter how full your schedule is, if you try really hard you can always fit some more things in it!"

"No," the speaker replied, "that's not the point. The truth this illustration teaches us is: If you don't put the big rocks in first, you'll never get them in at all."

What are the "big rocks" in your life, time with your loved ones, your faith, your education, your dreams, a worthy cause, teaching or mentoring others? Remember to put these big rocks in first or you'll never get them in at all. So, tonight, or in the morning, when you are reflecting on this short story, ask yourself this question: What are the "big rocks" in my life? Then, put those in your jar first.

---

① pitcher ['pɪtʃə] n.（一侧有柄另一侧有口的）罐，壶

② brim [brɪm] n. 边，边沿，边缘

③ eager beaver ['igə 'bivə] 做事异常卖力的人，雄心勃勃的人，竭力讨好的人

他再次称赞，“好！”随后端起一罐水往瓶子里倒，直到水升至瓶口边缘处。他看着全班，问大家：“这个实例能说明什么呢？”

一个爱出风头的学生立刻举手回答：“说明哪怕时间安排已经看似很满，只要你肯动动脑再加把劲，总能见缝插针地完成更多事情。”

“不对，”时间管理专家否定了他，“这不是我想说明的。这个实例教给我们的道理在于，如果先放进去的不是那些大石块，它们将永远没法再放进去了。”

生活中，你的那些“大石块”又是些什么呢？与挚爱亲朋共度的时光，你的信念，修养，梦想，还是一份可敬的事业，抑或是去教育引导他人？记住，要先放进这些大石块，否则就没有它们的空间了。那么今夜或明晨，当你品咂这个小故事时，请扪心自问，我生活中的那些“大石块”究竟是什么呢？然后，就把这些首先放入生活这只大容瓶中吧。

成长的代价

◎ Rubel Shelly

As an editorial in the Caledonian-Record of St. Johnsbury, Vermont, put it: "Friday night five teen-age girls at Danville High School became five young adults, and they did so with class." I thought you'd like to know the story.

The Friday night in question was January 11, 2002. The setting was a packed gymnasium just prior to the start of the **varsity**① game. The five girls were members of the Danville High School basketball team—four of them **starters**②. They weren't in uniform to play that night and won't be for the remainder of this season. They were there to explain why they had been kicked off the team.

They were there to own a serious **infraction**③ of team rules. They were there to support their coach's decision to take them off the team. They were there to let the town know there was a problem in their little community that needs to be addressed. And they did it with appropriate **contrition**④ rather than defensiveness.

---

① varsity ['vɑrsɪti] n. 大学；大学（或学院）体育代表队，校队

② starter ['stɑrtɚ] n. 参赛人；发令员；起始者（物），起始阶段

③ infraction [ɪn'frækʃən] n.（对规则、法律等的）违犯，违反

④ contrition [kən'trɪʃən] n. 悔罪，抱愧

美丽校训励我心

The United States Military Academy/West Point: Duty, Honor, Country.

美国军事学院/西点军校：责任、荣誉、国家。

鉴于佛蒙特州圣约翰斯柏瑞市发行的《加勒多尼亚纪事报》上的一篇社论曾这样写道，“本周五晚，丹维尔高中的五位花季少女在全班同学的见证下完成了自己的成人礼”，我想你一定很想知道这个故事的始末。

上文所提本周五晚的确切时间是2002年的1月11日。故事发生在拥挤的体育馆内，正值校际赛的前夕。这五个女孩是丹维尔高中篮球队的成员，其中四人是参赛队员。当晚，她们却不是要穿着队服打比赛，甚至之后的整个赛季她们都没这个资格了。她们站在那儿，是要向大家检讨她们为什么被球队除名。

她们站在那儿，当众承认自己严重触犯了队规；她们站在那儿，证实教练已将她们开除球队；她们站在那儿，是要让全镇的人对本地存在的问题引起足够重视。她们没有表现出任何抵触的情绪，而是始终怀着深深的

While school had been out for the Christmas and New Year's holidays, the girls had gone to a party with several of their friends. It was New Year's Eve. There was alcohol there. And the five girls all drank some.

Coach Tammy Rainville has a zero-tolerance rule on drugs and alcohol for the members of her team. Every kid who plays for her knows that rule. So when classes resumed after the break and accounts of holiday parties were shared, rumors about the five girls began closing in on them. Coach Rainville didn't have to confront them, for they got together and decided to go to her with the full story.

The coach said she couldn't back down on her policy. And the players—two juniors and three seniors—agreed. That Friday night in the gym was part of their public support of the coach's decision.

One of the seniors spoke last. "We hope you will understand that we are not bad kids. We made a mistake... What we did was definitely not worth it. We hope this event will make everyone open their eyes and realize that there is a big drug and alcohol problem in our community," she said. "And if you work with us to try to solve this problem, you will help us feel that we have not been thrown off our basketball team for nothing." The five left the floor to deafening applause.

The Danville High School girls' basketball team may not win another game this year. But they've learned something about personal responsibility, the effect of one's actions on others, and integrity that will serve them well throughout life.

懊悔之意。

由于在圣诞和新年期间学校放假，这几个女孩就跟朋友们出去派对了。那天正是新年前夜，派对上自然少不了酒，于是这五个女孩每人都喝了一些。

泰咪·瑞安维勒教练一直严禁队员饮酒或是吸毒，她手下的每位队员都知道这个规矩。因此，当假期结束学校复课后，派对的事就被大家传开了，关于五个女孩沾酒的传言更是沸沸扬扬。因此不需要瑞安维勒教练来找她们对证，这五个人就商量好来向她负荆请罪了。

最终，教练告诉她们，自己不能违背原则，只能按规定处罚她们。这几位队员都同意了，她们当中有两个在读低年级，而另外三个都是高年级学长。周五晚在体育馆上演这一幕，就是为了把教练的这一决定公之于众。

她们中高年级的一位最后做了发言，“我们希望在场的每一位都能理解，我们不是坏孩子。我们犯了错……并为此付出了惨痛的代价。希望这次的教训能让大家认识到本地存在着严重的毒品和饮酒问题，”她说。“如果你们大家能和我们一起携手努力解决这个问题，就等于是在向我们伸出援手，让我们感到自己没有被球队白白放弃。”五位女孩在震耳欲聋的掌声中完成了自己的“成人礼”。

也许在今年的篮球赛中，丹维尔高中女队不会再创佳绩了，但是女孩们却学会了如何肩负起个人职责，明白了自身行为对他人的影响，而正直诚恳必将成为让她们受用一生的品格。

One Girl Changed My Life
改变我一生的女孩

◎ Rose Risnik

My childhood and adolescence were a joyous outpouring of energy, a ceaseless quest for expression, skill, and experience. School was only a background to the supreme delight of lessons in music, dance, and dramatics, and the thrill of **sojourns**① in the country, theaters, concerts. And books, big braille books that came with me on streetcars, to the table, and to bed.

Then one night at a high school dance, a remark, not intended for my ears, stabbed my youthful bliss: "That girl, what a pity she is blind." Blind! That ugly word implied everything dark, blank, rigid, and helpless. Quickly I turned and called out, Please don't feel sorry for me, I'm having lots of fun. But the fun was not to last.

With the advent of college, I was brought to grips with the problem of earning a living. Part-time teaching of piano and harmony and, upon graduation, occasional concerts and lectures, proved only partial sources of livelihood. In terms of time and effort involved, the financial **remuneration**② was disheartening. This induced within me searing self-doubt and dark moods of **despondency**③. Adding to my dismal sense of inadequacy was the repeated experience of seeing my sisters and friends go off to exciting dates. How grateful

---

① sojourn ['so,dʒə:n] n. 逗留，旅居

② remuneration [rɪ,mjunə'reʃən] n. 酬报；偿还，赔偿；酬金，赔偿金

③ despondency [dɪ'spɑndənsi] n. 沮丧，泄气，失望

美丽校训励我心

Brown University: In God we hope.

布朗大学：上帝给你我信念。

在青少年时代，我度过了一段激情迸发的欢愉岁月——时刻想要展现自我、不断攫取自身才能、急于丰富人生阅历，无不是我无法止息的追求。在学校里，一切仿佛只为音乐、舞蹈和戏剧而存在，只有这些课程能带给我无限喜悦，而流连于乡间、剧院和音乐会更让我的身心为之震颤。当然还有书籍，那些大部头的盲文书时时陪伴着我，无论是搭乘有轨电车，还是等候在餐桌旁，抑或是打发睡前时光。

然而，一天晚上，在一次高中舞会上，一句我无意间听到的话瞬间刺痛了我年少无忧的心，“那女孩是瞎子，好可怜！”瞎子！这个难听的字眼指向的是黑暗，空茫，僵化和无助。我迅速地回转身，大声朝她喊去，用不着怜悯我，我的生活快乐得很。可是，快乐还是渐渐离我而去了。

随着大学生活的到来，我不得不开始为生计而奔波。课余时间为人教授钢琴及训练和声，逢到毕业时偶尔赶场演奏或讲演，所有这些放在一起也只够我勉强维持生活。与付出的时间和精力相比，我所收到的报酬实在是叫人灰心丧气。这也触动了我内心深处强烈的自我怀疑感，我就此变得阴郁消沉起来。一次次看到姐妹和伙伴们兴冲冲地外出赴约，自身缺陷为

I was for my piano, where—through Chopin, Brahms, and Beethoven—I could mingle my longing and seething energy with theirs, and where I could dissolve my frustration in the beauty and grandeur of their conceptions.

Then one day, I met a girl, a wonderful girl, an army nurse, whose faith and stability were to change my whole life. As our acquaintance ripened into friendship, she discerned, behind a shell of gaiety, my recurring plateaus of depression. She said, "Stop knocking on closed doors. Keep up your beautiful music. I know your opportunity will come. You're trying too hard. Why don't you relax, and have you ever tried praying?"

The idea was strange to me. It sounded too simple. Somehow, I had always operated on the premise that, if you wanted something in this world, you had to go out and get it for yourself. Yet, sincerity and hard work had yielded only **meager**[①] returns, and I was willing to try anything. Experimentally, self-consciously, I cultivated the daily practice of prayer. I said: God, show me the purpose for which You sent me to this world. Help me to be of use to myself and to humanity.

In the years to follow, the answers began to arrive, clear and satisfying beyond my most optimistic anticipation. One of the answers was Enchanted Hills, where my nurse friend and I have the privilege of seeing blind children come alive in God's out-of-doors. Others are the never-ending sources of pleasure and comfort I have found in friendship, in great music, and, most important of all, in my growing belief that as I attune my life to divine **revelation**[②], I draw closer to God and, through Him, to immortality.

---

① meager ['migɚ] adj. 瘦的；粗劣的，不足的，贫乏的

② revelation [ˌrɛvə'leʃən] n. 揭示，暴露；展现；(宗教)启示

我带来的失落感更是无以复加。幸好还有钢琴相伴，在肖邦、勃拉姆和贝多芬的乐声中，我炽烈的生命欲求与之交汇，恣意挥洒激情。我全部的失意沮丧也在他们美妙壮阔的音乐空间里彻底消融。

后来有一天，我遇到一位女孩，她是名战地护士，这个好姑娘即将用她的信念和坚定来改变我的人生。随着我们从相识到日渐熟络成为朋友，她觉察到我快意的外表之下是反复出现的情绪低落。她对我说："掩闭的门是敲不开的。何不迈进你美丽的音乐世界，只要你肯坚持下去，我相信机会终将眷顾你。你的神经一直绷得太紧了，不如先放松下来，你可曾做过祷告？"

完全陌生的概念，听起来像是坐享其成。不管怎么说，一直以来我做事都基于一个前提，如果在这个世上你想得到什么，那么你就得自己去拼搏、去实现。不过，既然之前的热情和努力都回报甚微，寻求别的途径又有何妨。怀着试试看的心态，我有意识地让自己养成每日做祷告的习惯。我向上帝告白："主，你将我带到这尘世，那么请指明我存在的意义。请赐福于我，让我成为有用的人，对得起自己和世人。"

接下来的几年里，我收到了上帝的回音，如此明确满意的人生答案显然超出了我最好的期盼。其中的一个回应来自"迷人山丘"，在那里，我和我的护士朋友有机会看到盲童们兴奋地回归大自然，投入上帝的怀抱。除此之外，朋友的情谊和伟大的音乐给我带来了无尽的欢乐和慰藉。最重要的是，我越来越坚定了我的信仰，每当我聆听上帝的神示时，我都感到自己正日益与他靠近，并经由他接近永恒。

Overcoming Shyness
战胜胆怯

◎ Linda Butler

I was a shy kid. To me, people were complex, intimidating, unpredictable, and unknown. I didn't even like to answer the telephone for fear I'd have to talk to somebody I didn't know. I enjoyed the solitude of exploring the golden California hills that were near my home. Winding along hills and streams was invigorating yet peaceful.

However, at school I had to spend all day in the company of others. My escape was reading. Reading was acceptable and it was solitary. Studying was another thing I could do quietly and by myself. I spent a lot of time studying and was rewarded with good grades. My one **downfall**① was Spanish—I'd get all As on my written work and tests, but Ds and Fs on the spoken part. I simply could not get up in front of the class to speak those simple dialogues.

Eventually I went to college. I realized that some people were rather fun to hang out with. Yet my childhood shyness carried over and I found myself tongue-tied and embarrassed whenever I found myself in a conversation.

During my third year of college, I decided that I'd had enough of being shy. I found that I enjoyed being around people and I wanted to be able to converse

① downfall ['daʊnˌfɔːl] n. 大阵雨，大阵雪；垮台，衰落

美丽校训励我心

Chicago University: Let knowledge increase so that life may be enriched.

芝加哥大学：益智厚生。

我是个胆小的孩子。在我看来，人都是那么的复杂可怕，莫测难懂。因为畏惧同陌生人说话，我甚至都不愿接听电话。我喜欢一个人到家附近的山间探幽，在那里，整个加州山脉呈现出一派金黄色。我沿着逶迤的山路和蜿蜒的溪流缓步而行，顿觉精神备至，心下安宁。

可是，在学校里，我不得不整天与人接触。我只好躲到书本中去。阅读可以，书页间的时光专属于我。或者做功课也行，亦能让我一个人安静地做事。因为我会花很多时间在功课上，所以我的成绩还不错。我唯一的弱项是西班牙语，所有的书面作业和测试成绩都是 A，唯独口语部分只拿到 D 和 F。其实想拿高分很容易，只要站在全班面前做一些简单的对话就可以了，但我就是没这个勇气。

后来，我上了大学。这时我才发觉，和有些人交往其实很有趣。不过，年少时胆怯的毛病还是没有改善，每当要开口与人交流时，我就舌头打结，面红耳赤。

大三那年，我实在受够了自己的这副样子。我愿意置身于人群中，并

freely like the other students around me. I resolved to change my outlook and behavior and overcome my shyness.

Along the way, I had learned a few words and phrases in several foreign languages—Spanish, German, and Russian. One day while on campus, I noticed an advertisement for positions on the local classical music radio station. I had grown up listening to classical music, and I loved it. I also realized that my language background enabled me to easily pronounce names such as Tchaikovsky, Albinoni, Chopin, Dvorak, and Rachmaninov.

In order to get a job at the radio station, applicants needed to submit an audition tape and be interviewed. My goal was merely to survive the interview and making the tape—going into a recording booth and reading advertisements and announcing symphonies and operas. I had absolutely no background in radio, and absolutely no hope of getting the job. The idea of talking to thousands of listeners in "radioland" terrified me. No, I didn't really want the job, I just wanted to know that I could speak onto a tape and talk to an interviewer.

I survived the interview. The station manager was soft spoken and had a wonderful mellow voice that made me feel calm and comfortable. The recording booth was a bit intimidating with all the gauges, buttons and flashing lights, but it was **intriguing**① as well. I was given brief descriptions of symphonies and a public service announcement to read, and a list of composers' names to pronounce.

It wasn't hard to read the descriptions and announcements, and the names, long familiar to me, were simple to speak. I left the recording session with a sense of relief that it was over, and a sense of accomplishment that I had actually done this strange and terrifying thing.

---

① intriguing [ɪn'triːgɪŋ] adj. 引起好奇心（或兴趣）的，有迷惑力的

且渴望像身边的同学一样与人交流自如。我下定决心要改变自己的人生观和处事方式，克服心中的胆怯。

在践行诺言的过程中，我还特意接触了多门外语，学会了像西班牙语、德语和俄语中的一些简单语汇。有一天在校园里，我注意到了一则当地一家古典音乐电台的招聘启事。我从小就喜欢听古典乐，可谓是一个古典乐迷。我还发觉，我浮薄的外语知识足以令我轻松念出诸如柴可夫斯基、阿尔比诺尼、肖邦、德沃夏克、拉赫玛尼诺夫等音乐家的名字。

想要获得这份电台工作，申请人必须递交一份试音磁带，还得接受面试。我的目标仅仅是获得面试资格，并灌录自己的声音——走进录音棚，对着话筒播读广告，放送交响乐及歌剧。我从未接触过播音领域，自然也没指望真能获得这份工作。我根本也没胆量对着“广播园地”频道的上千名听众发声。不要，我不是真想成为电台主播的，我只是想证明我能在磁带上呈现自己的声音，可以和面试官交流罢了。

我赢得了面试资格。电台主管说话间语态柔和，声音甜美动听，一下子就消除了我的紧张，让我感到镇定而放松。录音棚里布满了各类仪器、按钮和不停闪烁的指示灯，我感到有点害怕，但同时又充满好奇。工作人员交给我一份曲目简介和一张公众服务短讯让我播读，之后我还念了一份作曲家名单。

这些简介和短讯并不难读，而那些耳熟能详的名字在我念来更是得心应手。完成录音环节离开录音棚时，我才松了口气，这一切总算都过去了；与此同时，一种莫名的成就感油然而生，我真的做到了这件令我陌生又害怕的事。

I was even more terrified to discover, about two weeks later, that I had actually **landed the job**①. I was to work part time, at night and on weekends. I had to sit in the on-air studio, play recordings, and talk to thousands of unknown people throughout the state of Utah! I learned, too, that Saturday afternoons featured a listener request time. That meant I had to answer the phone and talk to people; noting, finding, and playing their requests.

It was a challenging job, but I grew to enjoy it immensely. I announced music to thousands of listeners in Salt Lake City and throughout Utah. In addition to announcing music and taking requests, I held contests, awarding free tickets "to the third caller". I recorded and aired public service and promotional announcements. I began to feel comfortable talking to these people, these strangers, who I couldn't even see.

It was a unique experience, being a DJ. After a few months, I realized that talking to people was not scary, but actually fun. I married and had five children. Speaking to people and navigating **bureaucracy**② became simple. Eventually I found myself in another job—interviewing people and writing their stories in a weekly community newspaper.

Although I now spend many hours each week talking with people, I'm still basically a quiet person. Perhaps it is my soft voice and my quiet nature that helps draw people out as they respond to my questions as I interview them. My former shyness is an asset, as I can relate to people who feel discomfort when they talk to this local newspaper reporter. I still enjoy moments of solitude and the peace found in nature. But I'm also glad I resolved to make a change in my life that has opened many doors and opportunities that I never knew existed.

① land the job 获得工作

② bureaucracy [bjʊ'rɑkrəsi] n. 官僚；官僚主义，官僚作风；行政系统，政府机构

更让我受宠若惊的是，两周后我竟得知自己被录用了。为此，我需要在晚间和周末到电台兼职。我就要坐进直播间，为大家播放唱片，还要对着犹他州数以千计的陌生人讲话！我还得知，每周六下午都是听众点歌的特别时间。这意味着我得接听电话并与听众交流，记录下他们想听的曲目，随后找出来为大家播放。

这是一份充满挑战性的工作，我却很快就乐在其中了。我在盐湖城向整个犹他州的数千听众放送音乐。除了常规的节目方式，我还设置了奖励环节，赠送免费门票给“第三位打进电话的听众”。我还录制并发布了有关公众服务及其推进的短讯。我开始自如地和听众互动，哪怕我们只是素未谋面的陌生人。

对于我来说，成为电台 DJ 真是一次独特的经历。几个月后，我再也不惧怕与人交流了，甚至觉得充满乐趣。后来我结婚成家，有了五个孩子。无论是与人交谈还是寒暄交际，对我来说都不再是什么难题。最后，我竟干起了记者这一行——我为当地一家周报做人物访谈，并撰写他们的故事。

尽管现在我每周都要花很多时间在谈话上，本质上我却仍是个话不多的人。也许正是因为我柔和的嗓音和这种安静的本性，才使得采访对象在面对我的提问时能够敞开心扉。而先前的胆怯亦成了我的财富，让我在采访当中能够及时顾及到他人的不安情绪。如今的我依然喜欢一个人独处的时光，喜欢在大自然中找寻平静。但我同样很高兴，我能下定决心转变自己，为我今后的人生开启了多重未曾奢望过的机遇之门。

Change
改变

© Kranthi Pothineni

Many say, I want change
Want change in my time
Want change in my life
I want a change badly
I want change, many say

They pray for a change
They wish for a change
They look for a change
But they will not change
They just wait for change

It never happens to them
It will never ever happen
By mere prayer or wish
It must start from inside
With tons of determination

总有人说，我要改变
时间要改变
生活要改变
我多么想改变啊
我要改变，总有人说

他们祈求改变出现
他们愿望改变降临
他们四处寻找改变
唯独自己墨守不变
但愿改变找上门来

改变却迟迟不来
永远不肯出现
谁叫你只会祈祷或是许愿
改变是要从心开始
坚定不移走下去

Change is not so easy
It takes lots of time
So it needs determination
The will to make change
The will to see change

Then only things will change
Then only time will change
Then only life will change
So go and get change
To see the bliss of change

改变没那么容易
付出时间
假以决心
勇于做出改变
勇于经受改变

如此才会真的改变
时间会改变
生活会改变
踏出这一步，转变这一切
让改变赐予你全部好福气

Chapter 3

搏击未来·追梦之路

The difference between the impossible and the possible lies in a person's determination.

可行与不可行的区别，来自于一个人的决心。

A Dream of Green Grass
绿茵梦

◎ Moraima Garcia

I was born in one of the poorest neighborhoods of Caracas, Venezuela. My dad was a truck driver and my mom was working in a mayonnaise factory when they met. Both had moved from the countryside looking for better opportunities, and in a way they found them. At least they had electricity in their new house.

Neither Mom nor Dad went to school, but Dad was an **avid**[①] reader and encouraged us to be like him, and they went to great lengths to make sure we did what they could not. I studied hard to make them proud. I was always number one in my class, teachers loved me and I loved learning new things every day.

By the time I was fifteen, we had discussed what I wanted to do when I grew up. Dad dreamed of me being a lawyer, but he was afraid corruption was too powerful in our country so he never insisted. He supported me when I decided to become a journalist.

Mom was very excited about my future too. One day she came home with a brochure from one of the most **prestigious**[②] colleges in the country, which happened to be located fairly close to our neighborhood. She was so happy—

① avid ['ævɪd] adj. 渴望的，热衷的

② prestigious [prɛ'stidʒəs] adj. 受尊敬的，有声望的

美丽校训励我心

California Institute of Technology: The truth shall make you free.

加州理工学院：真理赋予人自由。

我出生在委内瑞拉的加拉加斯，是那里贫民区的孩子。父母相识的时候，父亲是个货车司机，母亲在一家美乃滋工厂上班。为了寻求更好的机遇，他们都搬离了乡下，而后在某种程度上可以说他们找到了这个契机。至少，他们的新家通上了电。

父亲母亲都没有上过学，但是父亲却酷爱阅读，并且鼓励我们像他一样热爱读书。为了让我们能弥补他们的缺憾，他们不遗余力地付出辛劳。我更是努力学习，以期不负所望。我常常考取班里的第一名，老师很喜欢我，而我也乐于每天获取新的知识。

到了 15 岁那年，一家人一起讨论了我的未来——长大后我要做什么。父亲的愿望是我能够成为一名律师，但他同时又不免担心国家的腐败已经太成问题，因此并未坚持主张。当我决定要当记者时，他支持了我的想法。

对于我的未来，母亲也显得很积极。有一天，她带回家一份来自一所全国知名大学的宣传册，而这所大学恰巧离我们的位置很近。让她高兴的

they had a journalism school and the tests were just a few months away. We had to get ready!

I looked at her **dumbfoundedly**[1]. She couldn't be serious. That was one of the most expensive colleges in the country, and sometimes we barely had money to take the bus. I didn't say so though; I just told her I didn't want to study with some **snobbish**[2] kids who surely had no idea what real life was like. I wanted to go to a state college, where the people were more like me.

The only problem with that option was that the constant riots and strikes made it almost impossible to finish a degree there. People would study eight years instead of the five it was supposed to take because of all the time they lost during the never-ending political protests. We knew I needed to graduate quickly, so I could find a job and help out financially at home.

I tried to tell her it was impossible for me to be accepted. True, I had great grades, but journalism was the most sought-after degree, and there were thousands of people fighting for each place.

Mom said there was only one way to find out: by taking the admissions test. I fell back on my last argument—money. I explained what had been obvious to me since the beginning of the conversation. We could not afford it. At that point she smiled triumphantly and opened the brochure she had been holding.

Among the descriptions of the courses and facilities and other information was a very small paragraph indicating that there was a scholarship program. I decided to let her dream a little bit longer, and I agreed to submit my application. I didn't pay attention to the subject until the day of the admittance test. I have to confess I took the exam to humor my mom.

---

① dumbfoundedly [dʌm'faʊndɪdli] adv. 惊呆地，目瞪口呆地

② snobbish ['snɒbɪʃ] adj. 势利的，谄上欺下的；不懂装懂的，自命不凡的

是，这所大学设立了新闻学院，而考试就在几个月之后。我们得赶紧准备了！

我怔怔地看着她。这怎么可能，那可是全国最贵的学校啊，而我们有时连搭公车的钱都掏不起。然而我却没能这样说。我只是告诉母亲，我不想跟那些势利鬼一起念书，他们根本不了解生活的真实面目。我想上州立大学，那儿的学生和我才更接近。

唯一的问题是，如果这样选择，获得学位将是一件遥遥无期的事，持续不断的骚乱和罢工影响着学情。由于这种无休止的政治抗议所耗费的时间，本应五年完成的学业很可能会延长至八年。而我，需要尽快毕业，找到工作，帮助家里补贴家用。

我试图让母亲明白我是不可能被录取的。诚然，我成绩优秀，但新闻专业的学位炙手可热，竞争激烈到录取比例只有数千分之一。

母亲的回答却是，想知道自己行不行只有一个办法，那就是去参加入学考试。我只好搬出最后的理由——我们没钱。这一点从谈话的一开始对我来说就是心知肚明的。我们付不起学费的。母亲听到这却欣然自若地笑了，翻开手中的那本小册子。

在所有有关学校课程、设施介绍以及其他信息的内容间，夹杂了很短小的篇幅用以说明学校的奖学金计划。我决定让母亲的美梦做久一点，就答应她递交了申请。考试这天来临之前，我没在题目上费一点心思。我得说，我参加考试只是为了敷衍我母亲。

然而，第一份惊喜却从天而降，我在名单上看到了我的名字。我竟被

The first surprise came when I saw my name on the list. I was accepted! Only one other kid from my high school was accepted that year.

My dad, who is usually the most pessimistic person in the universe, was terrified. How were we going to pay the tuition? My mom used one of her typical answers, "I don't know, but we will. Even if we have to work day and night, our daughter is going to that college." Her determination was so strong we didn't dare say anything. It wasn't only my dad, though—my whole family thought we were just plain crazy. It was a college for rich people—how did we even think it was possible?

By this time, I was allowing myself to get excited by the idea. I knew a degree from that college would open doors that I never dreamed of, but I was still too afraid to get my hopes up. We filed the papers for the scholarship and for weeks we waited, wavering between eagerness and panic about what the answer might mean to us.

Finally I received the news. I got a scholarship that would cover eighty-five percent of the tuition for three years, and if I earned good grades they would give me a soft loan for the remaining two years that I could pay back once I got a job. What had seemed impossible only a couple of months ago was really happening. I was going to attend one of the most exclusive colleges in Venezuela.

I won't say college was easy. I did feel out of place most of the time. I had to borrow materials and books because we could barely find the money to pay the fifteen percent the scholarship didn't cover, much less for other things like books or photocopies. I had only one pair of jeans and two tops.

I did not go on vacation to Miami or Europe, but I still got good grades and met the best friends I could ever imagine. We would sit on the grass, which was always so green and fresh, and talk and laugh and study.

录取了！当年我的高中除了我之外，仅仅只有一个孩子考上了。

这时候轮到我的父亲——世上最悲观的人——开始感到慌乱。我们怎么才能拿得出这笔学费呢？母亲倒是用她那一贯的口吻坚定说道："虽然现在还不知道怎么办，但是我们一定能做得到。就算我们要不分昼夜地拼命工作，我们的女儿还是要上那所大学。"她强大的决心让我们无言以对。然而，不光是我父亲，一大家子的人都觉得我们真是疯了：那可是给富人准备的学校，根本就是我们连想都不该想的啊！

到此时，我允许我自己为这个消息而雀跃。我深知拿到那所大学的学位就等于打开前程的大门，那是我未曾奢望过的，所以我还是小心翼翼，害怕一切成空。我们填好了申请奖学金的所有材料，接下来就是数星期的等待，未知的命运让我们一度徘徊在热切和惶恐之间。

最终，我等到了消息。我获得了这份奖学金，它足以支付我三年当中学费的 85%，而且如果我的成绩优异，对于余下两年的学费，校方还可以为我提供一份低息贷款，只要工作后偿还即可。一切在若干个月之前还看似那么不可能，现在竟都成真了。我即将踏入全委内瑞拉最高学府之一的这所名校了。

进入大学之后的生活无法说是轻松的，很多时候我都感到不自如。家里勉强为我凑够了那剩余 15% 的学费，因而学习材料和教科书我只能靠借阅，更不消说额外的参考书和影印资料了。全部的衣服也只有一条牛仔裤和两件上衣。

尽管我没能去迈阿密或是欧洲度假，但我仍然取得了优异的成绩，结识了我认为最棒的朋友。校园里绿茵常新，我们席地而坐，或开怀畅谈，或钻研学问。

The day I graduated, I gave my mom the medal. We walked by the campus, with everyone smiling at us, my mom beaming. She was so proud. I remember telling her that if it weren't for her, I would have never even tried. In her characteristic nonchalant way she said, "Don't worry about it, baby. Even before you were born I would pass in front of this university every day on my way to work at the factory. And from the window of the bus I would see the mowed lawns and the students lying on the grass, and I would think: one day a daughter of mine is going to study there. You see? I just knew you would. I dreamed of this green grass too many times; it had to come true."

I found a good job after college, paid off my loan, and won another scholarship for a master's degree. I now work for an international company. I've traveled around the world. I'm moving to New York, and the time when I didn't have money for the bus seems really far away. But I never forget that it was my mom's dream that made me do what everyone thought was impossible.

毕业那天，我把奖章戴在了母亲身上。我们走过校园，迎着他人微笑的目光，母亲是那么喜气洋洋。她是如此的自豪。我记得自己告诉母亲，当初如果不是因为她，我可能根本就不会做出尝试。母亲用她特有的淡然回答："宝贝，这没什么。在你出生以前，我每天都会经过这所大学去工厂上班。透过车窗，我看到修剪平整的草坪，学生们躺在绿茵之上，那时我就在想，我的女儿有一天也要到那里去学习。看吧，我一早就知道你会的。我无数次憧憬的这个绿茵梦必将成真。"

大学毕业后，我找到了一份优越的工作，不仅还清了贷款，还赢得了攻读硕士学位的奖学金。现在我在一家跨国公司就职，常有机会满世界跑。我即将搬往纽约，那些没钱搭公车的日子已是太过遥远的记忆。但我永远不会忘记，是母亲的梦想，促使我实现了这被视为不可能的一切。

The Power of Determination

意志的力量

◎ Burt Dubin

The little country schoolhouse was heated by an old-fashioned, pot-bellied stove. A little boy had the job of coming to school early each day to start the fire and warm the room before his teacher and his classmates arrived.

One morning they arrived to find the schoolhouse **engulfed**① in flames. They dragged the unconscious little boy out of the flaming building more dead than alive. He had major burns over the lower half of his body and was taken to the nearby county hospital.

From his bed the dreadfully burned, semi-conscious little boy faintly heard the doctor talking to his mother. The doctor told his mother that her son would surely die—which was for the best, really—for the terrible fire had devastated the lower half of his body.

But the brave boy didn't want to die. He made up his mind that he would survive. Somehow, to the amazement of the physician, he did survive. When the **mortal**② danger was past, he again heard the doctor and his mother speaking quietly. The mother was told that since the fire had destroyed so much flesh in the lower part of his body, it would almost be better if he had died, since he was

---

① engulf [ɛn'gʌlf] v. 吞没，淹没；大口吞食

② mortal ['mɔrtl] adj. 终有一死的；凡人的；致命的，（临）死的

美丽校训励我心

Duke University: Knowledge and religion.

杜克大学：敬知仰信。

乡村小校舍靠一只老式的大腹煤炉取暖。小男孩每天都最早来到学校，生起炉火把屋子烤暖，等着他的老师和同学们陆续到来。

一天早晨，大家到校时意外发现校舍起火了，烈焰吞噬了小屋。当失去知觉的小男孩被人从火海中拖救出来时，已是奄奄一息了。他的下半身严重烧伤，即刻被送往附近的县医院救治。

病床上的小男孩面目全非，处于半昏迷状态。朦胧中，他听到医生和母亲的谈话。医生说，这孩子恐怕很难活下来。鉴于可怕的大火已经彻底烧毁了他的下半身，这个结局也许对他再仁慈不过了。

然而，勇敢的小男孩并不想死。他充满了求生的意志。结果他真的活了下来，连医生都感到惊奇。危险期过后，他又听到医生与母亲在低语，这孩子的下肢肌肉已经大面积烧伤，他今后要经受的磨难很可能会令他生不如死，因为他注定了这辈子都要下肢瘫痪，整个下半身丧失知觉。

又一次，这个勇敢的小男孩下定了决心。他不想一辈子残疾。他要走路。但不幸的是，他自腰部以下毫无活动能力。他细瘦的双腿悬垂着，几

doomed to be a lifetime cripple with no use at all of his lower limbs.

Once more the brave boy made up his mind. He would not be a cripple. He would walk. But unfortunately from the waist down, he had no motor ability. His thin legs just **dangled**① there, all but lifeless.

Ultimately he was released from the hospital. Every day his mother would massage his little legs, but there was no feeling, no control, nothing. Yet his determination that he would walk was as strong as ever.

When he wasn't in bed, he was confined to a wheelchair. One sunny day his mother wheeled him out into the yard to get some fresh air. This day, instead of sitting there, he threw himself from the chair. He pulled himself across the grass, dragging his legs behind him.

He worked his way to the white picket fence bordering their lot. With great effort, he raised himself up on the fence. Then, **stake**② by stake, he began dragging himself along the fence, resolved that he would walk. He started to do this every day until he wore a smooth path all around the yard beside the fence. There was nothing he wanted more than to develop life in those legs.

Ultimately through his daily massages, his iron persistence and his resolute determination, he did develop the ability to stand up, then to walk haltingly, then to walk by himself—and then—to run.

He began to walk to school, then to run to school, to run for the sheer joy of running. Later in college he made the track team.

Still later in Madison Square Garden this young man who was not expected to survive, who would surely never walk, who could never hope to run—this determined young man, Dr. Glenn Cunningham, ran the world's fastest mile!

---

① dangle ['dæŋgəl] v. 悬垂，悬荡；追逐；诱惑，吊胃口

② stake [stek] n. 篱笆桩，栅栏柱；刑柱；股份，利害关系

乎像是假的一样。

最终他获准出院了。母亲每天为他按摩萎缩的双腿，但是他的下肢还是没有知觉，不听使唤，毫无生命的迹象。然而，他决心要站起来走路的信念，还是一如既往的强烈。

当他不需要卧床时，他的生活起居只能倚靠轮椅。在一个阳光明媚的日子，母亲推着轮椅，带他到院子里呼吸新鲜空气。就在这一天，他挣脱了束缚，举身扑下轮椅。他拖着身躯，曳着无力的双腿，在草地上艰难爬行。

他一下一下匍匐着挪动到自家的白色栅栏处。他抓住围栏，使出浑身力气让身体直立起来。接着，他用上身抵住栅栏，一根木桩挨着一根木桩地攀援着，把全身向前拖动，执意想让自己走起来。他开始每天这样锻炼自己，直到整个院子的四周，硬是被他沿着围栏磨出了一条平坦的小径来。他只有一个信念，那就是要让双腿重新恢复生命力。

终于，经过日复一日的悉心按摩，凭着他钢铁般不屈的毅力和坚定不移的信念，他真的能够自己站立了。紧接着，他开始蹒跚学步，直到完全行走自如，直到最后健步如飞。

起初，他还是步行去学校，之后干脆跑步上学——只是为了脚下生风的快感。后来在大学里，他入选了田径队。

再后来，在麦迪逊广场花园，这个年轻人一举打破了 1 英里赛的世界纪录！谁能想到，这就是当初那个在火灾中死里逃生，几乎从此丧失站立机会，更别奢望还能奔跑的小男孩。凭着顽强的意志，如今的格兰・坎宁汉姆博士突破了他生命中的重重桎梏。

To a Different Drummer
击出我天地

◎ Lennox Lewis

"Come on—put up your hands and fight!"

I groaned. Why was this happening to me? My mother had said, "No fighting," right before I left the house. After coming from London, England, to Kitchener, Canada to live with her, I was starting a new life. During recess, this kid wanted to **scrap**[1] with me, and now it looked like I wouldn't even be able to get through my first day of school and keep my promise to my mum.

"Naw," I replied.

"You're just chicken," he yelled. "Is that it? Are you chicken?" The kid's red hair blazed in the winter sun and his freckles seemed to jump out of his pale skin. At twelve, I was tall for my age, but I was kind of skinny and **lanky**[2]. He was taller than me, and with his heavy parka on, he looked heavier than me, too.

"No. I'm not chicken. My mother just told me to stay out of trouble."

"I don't care...I want to fight with you, anyway." He pushed me in my chest. Then he put up his hands. "Come on!"

So, I hit him. Down he went into the snow. Other kids on the playground

---

① scrap [skræp] v. 争吵，打架

② lanky ['læŋki] adj. 过分瘦长的

美丽校训励我心

Imperial College London: Knowledge is the adornment and safeguard of the Empire.

帝国理工学院：用知识为帝国增光添彩、保驾护航。

“来啊，亮拳头来打我啊！”

我叹口气。为什么会遇到这种事？临出门前，母亲才刚嘱咐过我，“别跟人打架。”自从我离开英国伦敦，搬来加拿大的基奇纳与她同住，我就开始了全新的生活。课间休息时，这个男孩前来寻衅，看来连上学第一天都捱不过，我就要失信了。

“不想。”我回答。

“你就是个胆小鬼，”他大声嘲笑我，“没说错吧？承认你是胆小鬼了？”男孩的红头发在冬日阳光的映衬下分外晃耀，那张苍白的脸上颗颗斑点都似在雀跃欢呼。12 岁的我，比同龄人要高，却因为细瘦而显得狭长。他比我还要高些，穿着厚重的派克大衣，看上去自然也比我有分量。

“我才不是胆小鬼。只是我妈妈不让我在外面惹事。”

“我可不管……我就要跟你比试。”说着就朝我胸前推搡起来。然后他端起拳头，“来啊！”

无奈之下，我出了手。一拳下去，他就栽在了雪地里。操场上的其他孩子很快围拢过来。他站了起来，还在比划着拳头。我又一拳朝他挥去，

started to circle around us. He got up. He put up his hands—and I hit him again. He went down for a second time. All the kids were yelling, "Fight! Fight!" This time, I kept my hands up just in case someone else in the circle of kids wanted a taste of me, too. I waited, and the kid got back up again.

He walked toward me, stuck out his hand and said, "Shake. I just wanted to see how tough you are. Wanna be friends?"

I heaved a sigh of relief and shook hands with him. I figured that I would need a friend. The snow, strange country, new school, the way that people spoke—different from my London street slang—and being the only black kid for miles around, all of this added up to being a weird new world for me.

I was born in London, England, and lived there with my mother until I was about eight years old. My mum wanted to find a better life for us, so she went to Chicago, in the United States. She left me with friends in London until she got settled enough to send for me. Mum ended up not staying in Chicago but moved to a small town in Canada because she had a friend there who helped her get a good job.

Meanwhile, back in England, I was getting into trouble. I had always felt like an outsider, different from the other kids. They didn't want to play with me. That made me mad, so I got into fights and ended up getting expelled for being a danger to the other kids at my school. The people I was staying with were upset with me and felt they couldn't manage me. So, after living with them for almost two years, they sent me to a home for kids—kind of a boarding school. I lived there for a year. I felt alone and bored, the food was gross, and I really missed my mother. Finally, she sent for me.

My mum met me at the airport in Toronto with a smile on her face, a warm hug, and huge parka to put on. When we went outside the airport, there was snow

他再次被打倒在地。所有孩子都在起哄，“打他！打他！”这时的我拳头在握，只是以防围观的孩子里还有人想尝尝我的厉害。我等着，倒下的男孩却再次顽强地站了起来。

他向我走来，伸出手，“握手言和吧。我就是想领教下你的厉害，交个朋友怎样？”

我这才松了口气，和他握了手。我想我需要这个朋友。白雪皑皑，陌生的国度，新的学校，就连人们说话的方式都不同于伦敦的那些街头俚语，方圆数里更是见不到一个跟我一样的黑人小孩。所有这些合起来，构成了眼前新奇的世界。

我是在英国伦敦出生的，8 岁之前一直都和母亲生活在那里。为了让我们过上更好的生活，母亲在我 8 岁那年去了美国芝加哥。她把我托付给伦敦的朋友，想等她一切安稳后，再把我接过去。但母亲最后还是离开了芝加哥，搬到了加拿大的一个小镇，那儿有朋友帮她安排了一份好工作。

与此同时，在英国这边，我却麻烦不断。我总觉得自己是个外人，不像其他孩子有自己的家。他们不愿意和我玩。这种孤立让我大为恼火，为此和人大打出手，结果校方认定我是个危险分子，开除了我的学籍。而我寄居的那户人家也深感不安，觉得我很难缠。所以，在和他们一起住了将近两年后，我被送到一个私人托管所——类似于寄宿学校的地方。我在那儿又待了一年。生活孤单无聊，饭菜难以下咽，我极度想念母亲。最后，终于等到她派人来接我了。

妈妈在多伦多机场迎接我，微笑着给了我一个温暖的拥抱，还给我加上一件厚厚的防寒大衣。走出机场时，眼前白茫茫的，地上、车上，乃至

all over the ground, the cars—everything! I didn't know what it was. I asked my mum, "What is this?" I touched the snow and was amazed by how cold and **fluffy**[①] it was. It was different from anything I had ever seen before.

The weather was different, my school was different, the country was different, but some things were still the same—I was still getting into fights. Other kids picked on me about my accent, the color of my skin, my grades, or whatever. I was different, still left out. It didn't matter; I hated getting picked on, and I let them know it—with my fists. All through grades seven and eight, I was sent to the principal's office so often that he and I became friends. Instead of punishing me, he would counsel me. He told me that I would be better off using the energy I had in more positive ways and encouraged me to play football and basketball after school. He also suggested that I check out boxing—maybe I could learn to use my fists in a constructive way instead of being on the destructive path I seemed to be headed for.

Even though I was an outsider and a loner, I liked going to school dances. At one of the dances, some of the guys wanted to fight a group of guys from another school. We agreed to meet them on neutral ground—the police boxing gym downtown. We showed up, but they didn't. While we were hanging around waiting for them, one of the boxing trainers called out to me, "You, come over here."

I walked over to him and he asked me, "Do you want to go a few rounds with him?" He pointed to a guy getting into one of the rings. I was pretty full of myself and figured I could take him because he was small, so I said, "Sure, why not?"

I just couldn't hit the guy. He danced all around me while I tried to hit him.

① fluffy ['flʌfi] adj. 绒毛的，毛茸茸的；蓬松的；空洞的，肤浅的

所有一切都银装素裹！我不知这是何物。我好奇地问妈妈："这白色是什么？"我伸手摸了一下，惊奇地发现它竟是冰冷松软的，不同于我以往见过的任何东西。

气候变了，学校变了，国度变了，但有些事却没变——我还是天天打架。其他孩子会因为我的口音、我的肤色、我的学业，我的种种而歧视我。我依旧与众不同，还是被人孤立。不过没关系，我讨厌受挤兑，为此我会用我的拳头来教训他们。整个七年级至八年级，因为打架我成了校长办公室的常客，久而久之竟和校长成了朋友。他并不处罚我，而是给我忠告。他劝说我把精力用到益处，并鼓励我课后去踢足球或是打篮球。他还建议我去了解拳击运动——也许我能从中悟到如何正当积极地运用我的拳头，而不是像现在这样靠暴力解决问题，在歧途上越陷越深。

尽管我依旧远离人群，形单影只，我却喜欢参加学校的舞会。在一次舞会上，有几个家伙想要和一群外校生拼架，就择定了一个中立的地点——市中心的警署拳击馆。我们准时出现了，对方却没来。正当我们四下闲逛等他们时，一个拳击教练喊我："你，过来一下。"

我走过去，他指着其中一个刚进场的人问我："想和他打几回合吗？"当时我很自大，加上对手身形很小，我认为打败他应该不在话下，就满口应承，"好啊，比就比。"

我却根本打不到那家伙。无论我怎样出拳，他总能辗转腾挪地轻松避开。然后，我的鼻子就结结实实挨了那小个子一拳。这一拳不仅打得我鼻

Then that little guy really **connected**[1] with my nose. Not only did that make my eyes water, but it bruised my ego and made me realize that there was more to the sport of boxing than just swinging my fists. The coach put me into the ring with another fighter who was about my size, and I did pretty well. That was a moment of decision in my life. I remembered what my middle school principal had told me and everything clicked. The boxing ring was where I belonged.

All through high school, I played football, basketball, and soccer, and I was on the track team. But from that day on, boxing was the sport that I liked the most. Because it's an individual sport, it's more challenging and exciting to me. I found that I enjoyed the thrill of one-on-one competition. I also liked the fact that it was up to me whether I won or lost—that I was the determining factor. I think I've always been a competitor, and winning would give me a glow of satisfaction and a good feeling about myself. There was always a bad feeling if I lost, and I didn't like that. I wanted to win—every time.

I started training with the man who got me into the ring that first time. He became my boxing coach, friend, mentor, and a father figure for me to look up to. I learned that boxing is a sweet science where I could use my brain as well as my strength and size. I used my ability to focus under pressure. Under his training, I went from being a street fighter to a gold medal-winning Olympic champion.

Though I was basically an outsider, even as a little boy I wanted to be first in whatever I set my mind to. Once I went professional, I worked hard and got what I wanted. I have earned millions, but for me, it's not just about the money. I made my dreams come true. I did it my way. I stayed away from bad promoters and bad managers and upheld my integrity. Throughout my career, I have gained, regained, and retained the WBC and IBF heavyweight belts, the most prestigious

---

① connect [kə'nɛkt] v. [体] 成功击中

子发酸、眼泪打转，也瞬间击垮了我的全部自负，令我意识到拳击运动绝不只是挥挥拳头这么简单。教练又安排我和另一个差不多块头的拳手比试，这次我打得不错。那是我生命中决定性的一刻。我记起中学校长教育我的那番话，现在一切都该兑现了。我是属于拳击场的。

整个高中时代，我不仅踢足球，打篮球，玩橄榄球，还参加了田径队。但是从那天起，拳击成了我最喜欢的运动。它是一项个人运动，因此能带给我更多的挑战和乐趣。我发现自己很享受这种一对一对抗的刺激，也很乐于拳击比赛的输赢全靠我一个人——我就是决定因素。我总是充满斗志，胜利会为我带来满足感，让我感觉良好。我不喜欢输，那样我会觉得很糟。我希望自己能赢——百战百胜。

我开始受训于第一次带我进场的那个人，他后来成为我的拳击教练，亦是我的良师益友，一个父亲般让我景仰的人。我渐渐明白，拳击是一门美妙的科学，在利用我的力量和身形的同时，我还可以运用我的智慧来打比赛。我能在压力下集中精神，发挥出我的优势。在他的训练之下，我从一个街头霸王变成了奥运冠军。

尽管本质上我一直特立独行，但从孩提时起，只要我下决心去做的事，就一定会争做第一。成为职业拳击手以后，我刻苦训练，取得了满意的成绩。我赢得了数百万的奖金，但对我来说，成功的意义远不仅仅是金钱。我实现了自己的梦想。我用我的方式立足于拳击界。我避开那些图谋不轨的赞助商和经理人，一身正气。纵观我的职业生涯，我数度争霸、蝉联并成功卫冕 WBC（世界拳击理事会）和 IBF（国际拳击联合会）重量级金腰

in the boxing world. I want my place in history, and I know I will have it.

A couple of years ago, I was given the title, Member of the Order of the British Empire, an honorary title bestowed by Queen Elizabeth II for distinguished achievement. I have come a long way from being a brawling London street kid to the man I am today—the man that my mum raised me to be.

带，获得拳击界的最高荣誉。我希望自己能留名青史，我知道我做到了。

几年前，为了表彰我的卓越成就，女皇伊丽莎白二世为我颁发了大英帝国勋章，使我成为获此殊荣的一员。回望过去，我走了很长一段路，由一个伦敦街头的小混混成长为今天这个有价值的人，实现了母亲对我的期望。

One Bite at a Time

一口一口地吃

◎ Anonymous

Stephen was on campus to **enroll**[①] when I first met him. One summer day I was heading over to the administration building when I heard someone call my name. I turned around and saw Philip, one of our admission counselors standing with another young man. I walked over to them.

As Philip introduced me to the young man, he reminded him that he would be taking one of my General Education classes, Introduction to Biblical Literature.

Stephen looked at me. With a somewhat pained expression he asked if my class was going to be "hard." Would he be able to pass? I sensed he was **reconciling**[②] himself to failing before the opening day of classes.

We talked about what the class would cover and all the things he would be expected to learn. It is a course in which we will cram a lot of facts and details into one semester. As I talked, I saw Stephen's eyes getting big with fear.

Then I remembered a bit of classical Chinese dialog:

Question: "How do you eat an elephant?"

Answer: "One bite at a time."

I told him to approach his work that way. Do his assignments, all of them,

① enroll [ɛn'rol] v. 吸纳（成员），招生；征募，使入伍；登记，注册

② reconcile ['rɛkən,saɪl] v. 使和解，调和；顺从，安于，甘于

美丽校训励我心

University College London: Let all come who by merit most deserve reward.

伦敦大学学院：让所有最具价值的人汇聚于此。

第一次见到斯蒂芬时，他正在校园里做入学登记。那是夏季的一天，我去往办公楼时，忽听身后有人叫我。我转回身，看到负责新生工作的菲利普正和另一个年轻人站在一起。于是我朝他们走过去。

菲利普把我介绍给眼前的这个年轻人，顺带提醒他，他即将修学我的一门通识教育课程，即圣经文学入门。

斯蒂芬看着我，表情略带痛苦地问我，课程对他来说是否会很难，他能通过考试吗？我能感觉得出，还没等开课，他就已经认定自己要挂科了。

我们一起谈论了全部的授课内容，以及所有他需要掌握的知识点。这门课在学期内会有大量的客观事实和细枝末节需要死记硬背。谈话间，我注意到斯蒂芬的眼睛已经睁得老大，显然，他很恐惧这门课程。

于是我想到了汉语中的一小段经典对话：

问："怎样吃掉一头大象？"

答："一口一口地。"

我建议他在课业上仿效此法。对于布置下来的学习任务，要一次性全

and to get them in on time, rather than being overwhelmed at all of the work. I told him that most successful students I knew made a master calendar of all the assignments so they could plan their work load.

As the fall semester wore on, I learned more of Stephen's story. He had struggled in school. It had taken him longer to finish than most young people. Family members, including his mother, kept reminding him that he was a failure. But he kept at it and in the face of their **prophecies**① he got his diploma to the contrary. Now, in the face of their nay-saying he had enrolled in college. He told me that before coming to our campus no one had believed he had much potential.

Stephen didn't become an "A" student. He didn't make any honor rolls. In fact, he often found himself on academic **probation**②. One reason was that he never did real well on tests. Still, he managed to pass most of his courses by being in class every day, turning in all of his assignments on time and breaking down his studying into bite-sized digestible portions. By passing course after course he began to gain a measure of self-esteem. He was a great singer and he was on the school's cross-country team.

Every time I saw him on campus he would brighten up and say, "One bite at a time." Whenever he introduced me to one of his friends on campus, he would tell them that he was succeeding when he was supposed to be failing. His secret, he said, was that he was practicing what I taught him before classes ever started: "Take it one bite at a time."

On graduation day, he was **romping**③ around in his robe with a bright smile saying, "One bite at a time."

---

① prophecy ['prɑfɪsi] n. 预言

② probation [pro'beʃən] n. 试用（期），试读（期）；缓刑（期）

③ romp [rɑmp] v. 嬉闹；轻快地跑（或走）

部完成，不要拖沓，这样就避免被堆积下来的课业弄得晕头转向。我还建议他说，我所知道的好学生大多都会制定一份日程表来安排每天的时间，以便有计划地分配学习任务。

随着秋季学期一天天过去，我渐渐了解到斯蒂芬的情况。他一直在艰难求学，比起一般年轻人，他总要花更长的时间来完成学业。包括他妈妈在内的家里人，都始终认定他不会有什么出息。但他还是坚持不懈地努力学习，在家人的冷嘲热讽声中取得了文凭。现在，纵然他们仍是反对，他还是上了大学。他告诉我，在到这儿来之前，没有人相信他会有所作为。

斯蒂芬没能成为优等生，他也没能登上光荣榜。事实上，他常常需要经受校方设置的试读期的考验。一个原因就是他每次的考试成绩总是不太理想。但他仍然每天到教室上课，按时上交所有作业，并把课业化整为零，每次只量力学会其中的一部分。就这样，他成功通过了大部分科目的结业考试。如此这般过五关斩六将地一门一门考下来，他开始获得了一定程度的自信。他是个很棒的歌手，还加入了学校的越野队。

每当我在校园里碰到他，他都会很高兴地招呼我，“一口一口地。”无论何时他在校园里向朋友介绍我，都会说到他在课业上如何临危不乱巧妙过关。而他过关的秘诀就是，每逢修学一门课程之前他都会实践我的方法，那就是，“一口一口吃下去。”

毕业那天，斯蒂芬身着长袍，脚步轻快，脸上扬起灿烂笑容好似在说，“一口一口地。”

Hani

汉妮

© Jamie Winship

The day I met Hani Irmawati, she was a shy, seventeen-year-old girl standing alone in the parking lot of the international school in Indonesia, where I teach English. The school is expensive and does not permit Indonesian students to enroll. She walked up to me and asked if I could help her improve her English. I could tell it took immense courage for the young Indonesian girl in worn clothing to approach me and ask for my help.

"Why do you want to improve your English?" I asked her, fully expecting her to talk about finding a job in a local hotel.

"I want to go to an American university," she said with quiet confidence. Her idealistic dream made me want to cry.

I agreed to work with her after school each day on a volunteer basis. For the next several months, Hani woke each morning at five and caught the city bus to her public high school. During the one-hour ride, she studied for her regular classes and prepared the English lessons I had given her the day before. At four o'clock in the afternoon, she arrived at my classroom, exhausted but ready to work. With each passing day, as Hani struggled with college-level English, I grew more fond of her. She worked harder than most of my wealthy **expatriate**

美丽校训励我心

University of Michigan: Art, science, truth.

密歇根大学：艺术、科学、真理。

那天见到汉妮·厄玛瓦提时，她年方十七，是个害羞的姑娘，正孤单单地伫立在学校停车场。我是这里的英文老师。印尼的这所国际学校学费昂贵，从不招收本土的孩子。她向我走来，请求我帮助她提高英文水平。我看得出，这个衣衫有些褴褛的印尼小姑娘是鼓足了极大勇气，才敢当面向我求助。

“为什么想要提高英文呢？”我问她，满心以为她会回答说自己准备在当地的宾馆找份工作之类。

“我想去美国读大学。”她平静的声音里透着坚定。这份充满理想主义色彩的梦想让我为之动容。

我答应每天放学后义务帮她补习。接下来的几个月里，她每天 5 点就起床，搭公车去她就读的普通高中。在这 1 小时的车程里，她既要学习日常功课，还要准备我前一天留给她的英文内容。下午 4 点钟，她会准时出现在我的教室，不顾疲劳马上进入上课状态。随着日积月累，汉妮的用功让我越来越喜欢她了，她在啃相当于大学难度的英文课本。她要比我教的那些移居国外的学生刻苦得多。

[1]students.

Hani lived in a two-room house with her parents and two brothers. Her father was a building **custodian**[2] and her mother was a maid. When I went to their neighborhood to meet them, I learned that their combined yearly income was 750 US. dollars. It wasn't enough to meet the expenses of even one month in an American university. Hani's enthusiasm was increasing with her language ability, but I was becoming more and more discouraged.

One morning in December 1998, I received the announcement of a scholarship opportunity for a major American university. I excitedly tore open the envelope and studied the requirements, but it wasn't long before I dropped the form in despair. There was just no way, I thought, for Hani to meet these qualifications. She had never led a club or an organization, because in her school these things simply did not exist. She had no guidance counselor and no impressive standardized test scores, because there were no such tests for her to take.

She did, however, have more determination than any student I'd ever seen. When Hani came into the classroom that day, I told her of the scholarship. I also told her that I believed there was no way for her to apply. I encouraged her to be, as I put it, "realistic" about her future and not to plan so strongly on coming to America. Even after my somber lecture, Hani remained **steadfast**[3].

"Will you send in my name?" she asked.

I didn't have the heart to turn her down. I completed the application, filling in each blank with the painful truth about her academic life, but also with my

---

① expatriate [ɛk'spetri,et] adj. 移居国外的，被流放国外的

② custodian [kʌ'stodiən] n. 监护人；看管者，保管员；守门人，门房

③ steadfast ['stɛd,fæst] adj. 坚定的，不动摇的；固定不变的，不动的

汉妮同她的父母和两个哥哥挤在一间两室的房子里，父亲是守门人，母亲在做帮佣。当我去他们的居住地走访时，我才知道他们一家人一年的收入合起来也只有 750 美金，这连在美读大学一个月的费用都不够。汉妮的求学之情随着她语言能力的提高日益强烈，但我却越来越替她担忧。

1998 年 12 月的一天上午，我收到了美国一所重点大学设立奖学金的通知。我激动地撕开信封，取出里面的文件仔细研读申请条件，却很快就跌回到失望中去。汉妮没机会了，我深知她不可能达到这些条件。她显然从没领导过任何学生会或是社团，因为在她的学校里根本就不存在这样的组织。她也没有所谓的指导顾问，拿不出任何权威测试的高分成绩，她从来就没机会参加这样的考试。

但有一点，她的确比我见过的其他学生都更有决心。那天当汉妮进到教室时，我就把奖学金的消息告诉给了她，同时也向她说明了这个申请对她来说几乎不可能实现。照我的想法，我鼓励她对未来现实一些，不要一下子就想着去美国这么远大的事。即使我对她讲了这么一番严峻的话，她依然表现得很坚决。

“您能为我填写一份申请吗？”她问。

我不忍心拒绝她。我填完了整张申请表，每一个空白处都写着她求学生涯的真实困境，同时也写下了我对她超凡的勇气和毅力的赞赏。封起信封，我告诉汉妮她成功的几率微乎其微，接近于零。

在接下去的几周时间里，汉妮加大了她的英文课业量，同时我安排她去雅加达参加英语流利度测试。整个考试采用机考的形式，而在这之前，汉妮从未使用过计算机，这对她来说是个不小的挑战。连续两周时间，我

praise of her courage and her perseverance. I sealed up the envelope and told Hani her chances for acceptance ranged somewhere between slim and none.

In the weeks that followed, Hani increased her study of English, and I arranged for her to take the Test of English Fluency in Jakarta. The entire computerized test would be an enormous challenge for someone who had never before touched a computer. For two weeks, we studied computer parts and how they worked. Then, just before Hani went to Jakarta, she received a letter from the scholarship association. What a cruel time for the rejection to arrive, I thought. Trying to prepare her for disappointment, I opened the letter and began to read it to her. She had been accepted.

I leaped about the room **ecstatically**[①], shocked. Hani stood by, smiling quietly, but almost certainly bewildered by my surprise. The image of her face in that moment came back to me time and time again in the following week. I finally realized that it was I who had learned something Hani had known from the beginning: It is not intelligence alone that brings success, but also the drive to succeed, the commitment to work hard and the courage to believe in yourself.

---

① ecstatically [ɪk'stætɪklɪ] adv. 狂喜地，心醉神迷地

和她一起学习了计算机主件及基本操作。接着，就在汉妮即将去雅加达之前，她收到了来自奖学金申请委员会的信函。这封拒函来的太不合时宜了，我心想。安抚她做好心理准备，我便展信念给她听。结果，她被获准了。

我情不自禁地跳了起来，惊喜万分。汉妮站在那儿，微微笑着，反倒对我的喜出望外有些不知所措。那一刻她的面部表情定格在我的脑海里，在接下去的几天里反复重现。最后，我终于意识到，汉妮其实早就明白这个道理，而我却到此时方才领悟：成功并不仅仅取决于一个人的聪明才智，更需要心怀大志地奋发图强，矢志不渝地努力拼搏，勇敢无畏地相信自己。

Never Say Never

别说不可能

◎ Rosa Torcasio

I cannot remember a point in my life when I desired anything other than becoming a teacher. As a child, I played school with my little cousins and friends just so I could practice for my future career. But what I didn't realize as a child was how expensive my dream was. I came from a middle-class family, and it seemed as though we'd always struggled to make ends meet. My dream of attending the University of Connecticut seemed so out of reach, but I wasn't willing to settle for anything less.

In the beginning of my senior year in high school, I began applying to colleges, but in my heart I had already made my decision. The University of Connecticut was the one. But a huge **hurdle**① stood between me and my dream—lack of financial resources.

At first, I was ready to give up. I mean, who was going to give me, the average high-school girl, that kind of money? I wasn't the smartest person in my class, not even close; but my heart was in the right place, and I was determined. I knew that scholarships were only given to the really smart kids, or so I thought. I applied for every scholarship I could get my hands on. What did I have to

① hurdle ['hɚdl] n. 栏架，跨栏赛跑；障碍，难关

美丽校训励我心

University of Connecticut: He who transplants sustains.

康涅狄克大学：迁吾邦者愿其生生不息。

我想成为一名老师，在我的生命中，我从未如此渴望过一件事。小时候，我就喜欢和哥哥姐姐或是小伙伴们一起扮家家闹学堂，冥冥中预演着我的未来。只是那时的我未曾意识到我的梦想是多么昂贵。我出身于中产阶级家庭，一家人为了生活已是疲于奔命。我想上康涅狄格大学的梦想在现实中显得如此遥不可及，而一旦退而求其次，我又心有不甘。

高中的最后一学年伊始，我开始申请大学。在我心中，我早已有了自己的选择，我只想上康涅狄格大学。但是现实和梦想之间却横亘着巨大的障碍——没有资金。

起初，我准备放弃了。试想，谁会为我这么一个再普通不过的高中女生出这笔钱呢？我不是班上最聪明的，或许连聪明都算不上。但我品行端正，意志坚定。我知道奖学金只颁给那些真正出色的学生，至少我是这样想的。于是我尝试着申请了所有我能触及的奖学金，怎能平白就认输呢？我的指导顾问随后把助学金机制也推荐给了我，我同样递交了申请，但对

lose? And then my guidance counselor told me about the financial aid system. I applied, but I didn't think I would qualify for that either.

After the holidays, my friends started receiving their acceptance letters from colleges, and I eagerly anticipated mine. Finally, a letter arrived from the University of Connecticut. Feelings of fear and joy overwhelmed me, but I was ready. I opened the envelope with trembling hands as tears engulfed my eyes. I had done it! I had been accepted to the University of Connecticut! I cried for a while, feeling both extremely excited and afraid. I had worked so hard to get accepted; what if I was denied admission because of my financial status?

I had been working a full-time job, but that was barely enough to pay for tuition. My parents couldn't afford that kind of money, and I wasn't going to pretend that they could. I was the first person in my family who would attend a university, and I knew how proud my parents were; but it was impossible for them to finance my education. However, my parents are incredible people, and they taught me never to give up on my dreams, regardless of the obstacles that I encounter, and never to lose sight of what I truly want out of life. My parents were right, and I continued to believe in both myself and my dreams.

Months went by before I heard anything from the financial aid office. I assumed that I didn't qualify for aid, but I wasn't ready to lose hope yet. At last, a letter arrived. I opened it eagerly, but it was a **false alarm**①. The letter requested more information in order to process my application.

This happened over and over, and my hopes kept getting shot down. Finally, a **bulky**② envelope arrived. I knew this was the one that would determine whether or not I could attend college. I opened the envelope and could hardly

---

① false alarm 假警报；引起一场空欢喜的人（或事物）

② bulky ['bʌlki] adj. 体积大的，庞大的；肥胖的；笨重的

于能否获准这个资格，我还是没有把握。

假期过后，朋友们纷纷收到了来自各大学的录取通知书，我热切期盼着我自己的那一份。终于，我收到了由康涅狄格大学寄来的信函。瞬间我被害怕和喜悦之情同时占据着，但我做好了接受一切的准备。我用颤抖的双手撕开信封，顿时眼中噙满泪花。我成功了！我竟被康涅狄格大学录取了？！眼泪止不住地流下来，我的心中无比激动，却又异常担心。为了这一刻我付出了太多的努力，一旦真的因为资金问题被拒，我又将何去何从?

我做了一份全职工作，但也仅够交齐我的学费。我的父母负担不了这些，我也不想以此为难他们。我是家里第一个考上大学的孩子，我知道父母心里有多自豪，可他们却苦于囊中羞涩无法供我读书。然而，我的父母却有着惊人的魄力，他们教导我，即使困难重重也不能轻易放弃梦想，不能忽略生命中真正的追求。父母是正确的，我依然相信自己，相信梦想终能实现。

几个月过去了，我仍然没有收到任何来自助学办公室的回音。我想自己大概是没有申请下来，但我仍然没有失去希望。最后，我终于收到一封信函，我迫不及待地展开，读来才知是空欢喜，来信的目的只是让我补充所需信息，以便申请程序能够得以继续。

如此这般反复几次后，我开始感觉希望渺茫了。最终，沉甸甸的一只大信封送到了我的手上，我知道关键的一刻到了，这封信将决定我能否进入大学。我取出信封中的文件，却几乎看不懂其间的意思。

第二天，我连忙把这些文件带到学校，拿给我的指导顾问请他帮我看看。当他从纸间抬起头来时，脸上绽放出灿烂的笑容。他告诉我，我不仅

understand what any of the documents inside meant.

The following day, I brought the documents to school and asked my guidance counselor to take a look at them. He looked up at me with a huge smile on his face and told me that not only was financial aid going to help me out with my expenses, but I had also won two of the scholarships I had applied for. I was in shock at first, then I cried. I had actually made my dream come true.

I am now a junior at the University of Connecticut, pursuing a degree in English. In the beginning of the new **millennium**[1], my dream will become a reality. I will be a teacher.

I live by this quote: "Reach for the sky because if you should happen to miss, you'll still be among the stars."

① millennium [mə'lɛniəm] n. 一千年，千年期；千禧年；未来人类的幸福时代，太平盛世

获得了减轻生活费用的助学金，同时还拿到了两份已申请的奖学金。一时我惊呆了，随后眼泪就夺眶而出。我真正在这一刻实现了我的梦想。

如今我已是康涅狄格大学的大三学生，攻读的是英语专业。千禧之初，我心中追寻的那个梦就要化作现实了。我即将成为一名老师。

我始终坚信这样一句箴言：“心存高远，若不得凌云志，尚可同群星辉。”

24 Things to Always Remember
常记在心的二十四行

◎ Matthew Quinata

Your presence is a present to the world
You are unique and one of a kind
Your life can be what you want it to be
Take the days just one at a time

Count your blessings, not your troubles
You will make it through whatever comes along
Within you are so many answers
Understand, have courage, be strong

Do not put limits on yourself
So many dreams are waiting to be realized
Decisions are too important to leave to chance
Reach for your peak, your goal and you prize

Nothing wastes more energy than worrying
The longer one carries a problem the heavier it gets

你的降临是赠予世间的礼物
你那么与众不同，那么独一无二
人生任由你去书写
认真过好每一天

惜福忘忧
宠辱不惊
究竟自在心间
通达，勇敢，坚强

放开手脚
无数梦想待你实现
抉择关头莫要坐失良机
攀向顶峰，达成目标，实现价值

伤神莫过忧思最
问题愈拖愈严重

Do not take things too seriously

Live a life of serenity, not a life of regrets

Remember that a little love goes a long way

Remember that a lot goes forever

Remember that friendship is a wise investment

Life's treasures are people together

Realize that it is never too late

Do ordinary things in an extraordinary way

Have health and hope and happiness

Take the time to wish upon a star

And do not ever forget

For even a day

How very special you are!

凡事切勿太较真
平静生活，别留遗憾

记住点滴爱意可以长流心田
记住全心全意换得永生永世
记住友情不生金却更胜似金
生命的财富即是人心的凝聚

要知道永远都不言晚
从平凡中创造不平凡
拥有健康，充满希望，心怀幸福
有时间就对着星星许个愿吧

永远不要忘记
哪怕一天
你是多么地特别！

采撷风致·趣事漫谈

That it's those small daily happenings that make life so spectacular.

正是每天上演的一幕幕小事让生活如此多姿多彩。

A Different Kind of Homework for Singapore Students: Get a Date
我们约会吧——新加坡学生的另类作业

© Seth Mydans

It was like a college **mixer**[1], a classroom full of young men and women seeking a recipe for romance. They had assembled for the first class of "Love Relations for Life: A Journey of Romance, Love and Sexuality." There was giggling and **banter**[2] among the students, but that was all part of the course as their teacher, Suki Tong, led them into the basics of dating, falling in love and staying together.

The course, in its second year at two **polytechnic**[3] institutes, is the latest of many, mostly futile, campaigns by Singapore's government to get its citizens to mate and **multiply**[4]. Its popularity last year has led to talk of its expansion through the higher education system.

"We want to tell students, 'Don't wait until you have built up your career,' " said Yu-Foo Yee Shoon, the Minister of State for Community Development, Youth and Sports, at a news conference in March. "Sometimes, it is too late, especially for girls."

---

① mixer ['mɪksɚ] n. 搅拌器；调酒师，调酒用的饮料；混频器，调音员；交谊会
② banter ['bæntɚ] n. 戏谑，逗笑
③ polytechnic [ˌpɑli'tɛknɪk] n. 理工学院，工艺专科学院
④ multiply ['mʌltəˌplaɪ] v. 乘，使相乘；(使)大大增加；繁殖

美丽校训励我心

Emory University: The prudent heart will possess knowledge.

埃默里大学：明辨之心善学。

眼前的场景犹如大学联谊会，教室里挤满了到此寻求恋爱秘籍的青年男女。他们聚在这里上的第一堂课即是《建立终身的恋爱关系：求爱、相爱、性爱之旅》。课堂上，不时有学生嬉笑或是彼此打趣，但这正是这门课的一部分，而唐舒绮老师正在向大家教授如何通过约会步入爱河，到日后朝夕相处的基本技巧。

新加坡政府近几年开展了多项国民运动，旨在促进新婚生育，实现本国人口上涨，但大都收效甚微，而在大学里增设这门爱的课程，是政府出台的又一新举，已在两所理工学院试行一年，如今是第二个年头了。而过去这一年间，这门课大受好评，以致引发讨论是否要将其在高校系统内进一步推广。

“我们想告诉同学们的是，‘不要等到立业再成家’，”身为新加坡社会发展部内务部长、专事青年及运动相关工作的符喜泉女士，在今年3月举行的记者招待会上说道，“尤其对女孩子来说，有时候会为时已晚。”

The courses are an extension of government matchmaking programs that try to address the twin challenges embodied in a falling birthrate: too few people are having babies, and too few of those who are belong to what Singapore considers the genetically desirable educated elite.

Last year Singapore's fertility rate fell to a record low of 1.24 children per woman of child-bearing age, one of the lowest in the world. It was the 28th year in a row Singapore had stayed below the rate of 2.5 children needed to maintain the population.

But even a replacement-level rate would not be enough for today's planners. The government recently announced that it was aiming to increase the population by more than 40 percent over the next half-century, to 6.5 million from the current 4.5 million.

"Teaching our youth in school how to fall in love" is a good solution, wrote Andy Ho, a senior writer at The Straits Times, a government-friendly newspaper that does its best to help out in Singapore's many campaigns.

In 1991, for example, when the government began offering cash bonuses to couples with more than two children, the newspaper printed tips for having sex in the back seat of a car, including directions to some of the "darkest, most secluded and most romantic spots" for parking. It suggested covering the windows with newspapers for privacy.

这类课程是政府所设牵线搭桥项目的又一延伸，旨在引起公众重视生育率下降问题，这其中体现了双重困境：愿意生育的夫妇太少；愿意生育的夫妇又很少出自受教育的精英阶层，这是为新国基因优选考虑。

新加坡去年的人口出生率跌至历史最低点，为人均 1.24 个孩子，排名世界倒数。而要想维持其人口现状，至少要达到人均 2.5 个孩子，而新国已经连续 28 年低于这一水平。

但新加坡当今的规划者并不满足于仅仅将人口维持在置换水平。政府最近宣布，其目标是在未来 50 年里实现人口数量超 40% 增长，争取从目前的 450 万增至 650 万。

《海峡时报》的资深作者何安迪就曾写道，“教导年轻学子如何谈情说爱”是个好出路。该报长期以来都是倒向政府的，竭力为新国的众多运动摇旗呐喊。

譬如在 1991 年时，政府曾提出向生育两个孩子以上的夫妇颁发奖金，该报立时刊出小贴士，教导大家如何在汽车后座上恩爱，包括有技巧地选择那些“最幽暗僻静同时又最具浪漫气息的地点”停车，还建议大家用报纸遮挡车窗，免受干扰。

The Campus as Runway
校园也 T 台

◎ Ruth La Ferla

Julia Flynn was darting to her classes at Columbia University last week in a Marc by Marc Jacobs daisy-patterned dress and high-heeled Chloé boots, her polished turnout accessorized with a Starbucks venti latte. "I'm really loving the whole Chanel, Valentino and McQueen shows," she said. "They completely inspired me." She had **gleaned**[①] her information that very morning from Style.com.

Ms. Flynn, 24 and a sophomore, is one in a small but self-aware and increasingly vocal **contingent**[②] of college women who dress to impress. The campus is their runway, a place to show off a style sense that is derived in part from their friends but more often attained through a click of a mouse, a gesture that affords them instant access to the once **arcane**[③] universe of fashion shows and to the style blogs and shopping sites, so many to imbibe with their morning brew.

If at one time college women subscribed to a regionally prescribed

---

① glean [glin] v. 拾落穗；仔细收集，耐心搜集；查明，弄清

② contingent [kən'tɪndʒənt] n. 分遣队，代表团；偶然事件；分得部分，份

③ arcane [ɑr'ken] adj. 神秘的，秘密的

美丽校训励我心

Northwestern University: Whatsoever things are true.

西北大学：凡其有实。

上周，哥伦比亚大学学生朱莉娅·弗里恩风风火火跨进教室，她身著马克·雅可布之马克雏菊碎花裙，脚蹬珂洛艾伊高跟长靴，这番精心修饰的亮相自然不忘配上星巴克超大杯拿铁做点缀。“我很追捧整季香奈儿，华伦天奴和麦昆时装秀，”她说，“它们给了我很多灵感。”这个年轻女孩当天早晨刚刚登陆 Style.com，搜罗了最新的时尚资讯。

今年 24 岁的弗里恩是一名大二学生，属于校园女生中为数不多、但却极具自我意识的时尚达人群体，这一群体的声势正日渐壮大。她们把校园当 T 台，秀出时尚个性，这一方面借鉴自她们的朋友，但更多的则是得益于互联网这个平台。只消动一动鼠标，她们就可以追踪到各类大牌时装秀，深入原本神秘的高端时尚领域，更可以登录时尚博客，搜索各类网店，信息纷繁足可以令她们在清晨的咖啡时间好好为自己充电。

如果说曾经的校园女生在着装方面倾向于区域性统一——东部地区都

uniform—twin sets and loafers in the East, frayed jeans and ponchos farther west—now, thanks to the democratizing influence of the Web, trends are **disseminated**① at warp speed, traversing regional borders and, paradoxically, encouraging a more individualized approach to dress.

Whether students' tastes run to an **urbanely**② preppie composite of mannish shirts, slim skirts and blazers, flowered dresses and Ferragamo flats, or to a cutting-edge pastiche of long loose-fitting sweaters, calf-length skirts and platform booties, their absorption with fashion points to a sea change, suggesting that the style bar has been raised, reaching a level of sophistication all but unknown a mere decade ago.

"The stereotype used to be that college students live in sweat pants and don't care about fashion," said Zephyr Basine, the editor of Collegefashion.net, a blog written by college women. "But today that isn't so." If at one time coeds signaled their cool by a kind of willful **dishevelment**③, arriving for 8 a.m. classes in trench coats tossed over pajamas, today that sort of carelessness marks them as out of touch.

"People now put more thought into what they're wearing," said Amy Levin, 24, a recent graduate of Indiana University and editor of Collegefashionista.com, an influential blog. "Getting ready for class is important. Students want to up their game. That means looking a little more serious, not just throwing on a graphic T-shirt and jeans."

---

① disseminate [dɪ'sɛmə,net] v. 散布，传播

② urbanely [ə:'benlɪ] adv. 彬彬有礼地，温文尔雅地

③ dishevelment [dɪ'ʃɛvəlmənt] n. 凌乱，衣冠不整

是两件套毛衣和平跟船鞋，到了大西部就流行破洞牛仔裤和斗篷装束，现在一切都大不同了。由于网络的大众化影响，潮流一经出现就会跨越地域界限迅速传播，结果却看似矛盾地熏陶出了更具个性化的穿衣风格。

尽管学生们的品味各不相同，有人喜欢温文不造作的装扮，如中性气质的衬衫、修身短裙搭配休闲小西装，或者印花连衣裙搭一双菲拉格慕平底鞋，也有人喜欢前卫出挑的混搭风，超大宽松的毛衣配一条长及小腿的筒裙，再穿上一双高防水台踝靴。这种与时尚的极度融合体现出一种巨变，表明时尚已经突破阻碍，在短短十年间就达到了令人难以想象的精细程度。

“成天穿着运动长裤，不知时尚为何物，这是长久以来关在象牙塔里的学生给大家留下的印象，” Collegefashion.net 的主编泽弗·巴辛说道，这是一个由大学女生原创的时尚博客。“现在一切都遭到了颠覆。”曾几何时，刻意不修边幅成为男女同校生扮酷之风尚，在睡衣外把军款风衣潇洒一披，就这么奔进教室上早 8 点的课。这种随性的装扮如今只能是一种落伍的表现。

24 岁的艾米·莱文说：“人们现在都爱在穿著打扮上花心思，”她刚从印第安纳大学毕业，同时也是另一个颇具影响力的时尚博客 Collegefashionista.com 的网站编辑。“精心打扮一番再去上课早已成为重头戏，学生们都想抢风头，让自己看起来更庄重，而绝不只是匆匆套上印花 T 恤和牛仔裤就出门。”

Love Is a Fallacy (Ⅰ)
爱是谬误（1）

◎ Max Shulman

Cool was I and logical. Keen, calculating, perspicacious, acute and astute—I was all of these. My brain was as powerful as a **dynamo**①, precise as a chemist's scales, as penetrating as a scalpel. And—think of it!—I only eighteen.

It is not often that one so young has such a giant intellect. Take, for example, Petey Bellows, my roommate at the university. Same age, same background, but dumb as an ox. A nice enough fellow, you understand, but nothing upstairs. Emotional type. Unstable. Impressionable. Worst of all, a faddist. Fads, I submit, are the very negation of reason. To be swept up in every new craze that comes along, to surrender oneself to idiocy just because everybody else is doing it—this, to me, is the **acme**② of mindlessness. Not, however, to Petey.

One afternoon I found Petey lying on his bed with an expression of such distress on his face that I immediately diagnosed appendicitis. "Don't move," I said, "Don't take a laxative. I'll get a doctor."

"Raccoon," he mumbled thickly.

"Raccoon?" I said, pausing in my flight.

"I want a raccoon coat," he wailed.

---

① dynamo ['daɪnə,mo] n. 发电机；精力充沛的人

② acme ['ækmi] n. 最高点，顶点，极点；鼎盛时期，顶峰阶段

美丽校训励我心

University of Edinburgh: The learned can see twice.

爱丁堡大学：智者能够透过现象看本质。

冷静如我，长于逻辑。敏捷、精明、睿智、尖刻、机灵，这些词汇构成了我的全部。我的大脑像电机一样发达，像化学家的天平一样精准，像手术刀一样犀利。想想看吧！我才 18 岁而已。

年纪轻轻就智力超群的人可不常有。就拿我的大学室友彼蒂·贝勒斯来说吧，同样的年龄相同的经历，却笨得像头牛。从外表看上去，小伙子无可挑剔，可惜脑子里却空空如也。意气用事，反复无常，缺乏主见。更要命的是，爱赶时髦。时髦这东西，在我看来毫无理智可言。不管流行什么，都一股脑地跟风，大家怎样自己就怎样，完全没脑子——要我说，这简直愚不可及。但是彼蒂可不这么想。

一天下午，我看见彼蒂躺在床上，脸上一幅痛苦不堪的表情，我立马断定他是得了阑尾炎。“别动弹，”我说，“也别吃什么泻药，我这就叫医生来。”

“浣熊。”他依稀咕哝着。

“浣熊？”我重复了一声，连忙刹住脚步。

“我要浣熊皮大衣。”他大声嚎啕。

我明白了，他不是身体不适，而是精神痛苦。“要浣熊皮大衣干嘛？”

I perceived that his trouble was not physical, but mental. "Why do you want a raccoon coat?"

"I should have known it," he cried, pounding his temples. "I should have known they'd come back when the Charleston came back. Like a fool I spent all my money for textbooks, and now I can't get a raccoon coat."

"Can you mean," I said incredulously, "that people are actually wearing raccoon coats again?"

"All the Big Men on Campus are wearing them. Where've you been?"

"In the library," I said, naming a place not frequented by Big Men on Campus.

He leaped from the bed and paced the room. "I've got to have a raccoon coat," he said passionately. "I've got to!"

"Petey, why? Look at it rationally. Raccoon coats are unsanitary. They shed. They smell bad. They weigh too much. They're unsightly. They—"

"You don't understand," he interrupted impatiently. "It's the thing to do. Don't you want to be in the swim?"

"No," I said truthfully.

"Well, I do," he declared. "I'd give anything for a raccoon coat. Anything!"

My brain, that precision instrument, slipped into high gear. "Anything?" I asked, looking at him narrowly.

"Anything," he affirmed in ringing tones.

I stroked my chin thoughtfully. It so happened that I knew where to get my hands on a raccoon coat. My father had had one in his undergraduate days; it lay now in a trunk in the attic back home. It also happened that Petey had something I wanted. He didn't have it exactly, but at least he had first rights on it. I refer to his girl, Polly Espy.

“我早该知道，”他哭喊着，不住地捶打太阳穴，“查尔斯顿舞卷土重来时我就该知道它们又会时兴起来。可我却像个傻瓜把钱都花在了课本上，现在我拿什么买浣熊皮大衣啊。”

“你是说，”我表示怀疑地问道，“人们真的又开始穿浣熊皮大衣了？”

“没看见校园里那些潮人都在穿嘛。你都去哪混了？”

“泡图书馆。”我交代了个貌似不受潮人欢迎的地方。

他从床上一跃而起，在房间里踱来踱去。“我一定得弄到一件浣熊皮大衣，”他显得很激动，“非到手不可！”

“彼蒂，这又何必呢？理智地想想看。浣熊皮大衣不太卫生，还掉毛，还有味道，还很笨重，还不怎么好看，还……”

“你根本不懂，”他不耐烦地打断了我，“现在的法宝就是它。难道你不想跟上潮流吗？”

“不想。”我实话实说。

“好吧，我可想着呢，”他肯定地说，“我愿意拿一切来换一件浣熊皮大衣。一切！”

我的大脑如同精密仪器，即刻高速运转起来。“一切？”我仔细打量着他。

“一切。”回答干脆响亮。

我若有所思地抚了抚下巴。巧了，我知道上哪能弄到一件浣熊皮大衣。我父亲读大学时穿过那么一件，现在正躺在我家阁楼的衣箱底呢。更巧的是，彼蒂刚好也有我想要的。尽管他还不算是拥有，但至少他是有优先权的。我说的是他的女朋友波莉·埃斯皮。

我觊觎波莉·埃斯皮已经很久了。我得强调下，我向往这位妙龄女郎可不是出于动了感情。的确，她是那种会让人心动的姑娘，但我绝不是那

I had long **coveted**[1] Polly Espy. Let me emphasize that my desire for this young woman was not emotional in nature. She was, to be sure, a girl who excited the emotions, but I was not one to let my heart rule my head. I wanted Polly for a shrewdly calculated, entirely **cerebral**[2] reason.

I was a freshman in law school. In a few years I would be out in practice. I was well aware of the importance of the right kind of wife in furthering a lawyer's career. The successful lawyers I had observed were, almost without exception, married to beautiful, gracious, intelligent women. With one omission, Polly fitted these specifications perfectly. Beautiful she was. Gracious she was. Intelligent she was not. In fact, she veered in the opposite direction. But I believed that under my guidance she would smarten up. At any rate, it was worth a try. It is, after all, easier to make a beautiful dumb girl smart than to make an ugly smart girl beautiful.

"Petey," I said, "are you in love with Polly Espy?"

"I think she's a keen kid," he replied, "but I don't know if you'd call it love. Why?"

"Do you," I asked, "have any kind of formal arrangement with her? I mean are you going steady or anything like that?"

"No. We see each other quite a bit, but we both have other dates. Why?"

"Is there," I asked, "any other man for whom she has a particular fondness?"

"Not that I know of. Why?"

I nodded with satisfaction. "In other words, if you were out of the picture, the field would be open. Is that right?"

"I guess so. What are you getting at?"

① covet ['kʌvɪt] v. 贪求，觊觎

② cerebral ['sɛrəbrəl] adj. 脑的，大脑的；运用理智的，诉诸理性的，非感情方面的

种会让情感占据理智的人。我想得到波莉是经过了深思熟虑、完全理智的衡量。

我现在是法学院一年级学生，过不了几年就要独挡一面。我深知，一个合适的妻子对律师的前途来说至关重要。据我观察，凡事业有成的律师大都会找一位美丽优雅而又聪慧的妻子来辅助自己。抛开一点不看，波莉堪称最佳人选。美丽非她莫属。优雅她亦兼备。唯独缺乏智慧。事实上她完全背道而驰。但我相信，假以我的调教，她会开窍的。不管怎么说，这都值得一试，毕竟，改造一个有姿色的笨女人，要比让一个有脑子的丑女人变漂亮来得容易吧。

“彼蒂，”我开口了，“你在和波莉·埃斯皮谈恋爱吗？”

“我觉得这姑娘很迷人，”他回答，“但我不知道这是不是你所谓的恋爱。干嘛？”

“那么，”我接着问，“你和她之间有认真吗？我是说，你们有没有确定关系或类似这种？”

“没有，我们只是常常见面，但我们各自也都有别的约会。干嘛？”

“有没有，”我兀自问下去，“某个她特别钟情的人？”

“据我所知是没有的。干嘛？”

我满意地点了点头。“那也就是说，一旦你让位，她身边就没人了。对吧？”

“我想是吧。你到底要干嘛？”

“没，没什么。”我若无其事地应着，从壁橱里拖出手提箱。

“你去哪儿啊？”彼蒂问我。

"Nothing, nothing," I said innocently, and took my suitcase out the closet.

"Where are you going?" asked Petey.

"Home for weekend." I threw a few things into the bag.

"Look," I said to Petey when I got back Monday morning. I threw open the suitcase and revealed the huge, hairy, gamy object that my father had worn in his Stutz Bearcat in 1925.

"Holy Toledo!" said Petey reverently. He plunged his hands into the raccoon coat and then his face. "Holy Toledo!" he repeated fifteen or twenty times.

"Would you like it?" I asked.

"Oh yes!" he cried, clutching the greasy pelt to him. Then a **canny**[①] look came into his eyes. "What do you want for it?"

"Your girl." I said, mincing no words.

"Polly?" he said in a horrified whisper. "You want Polly?"

"That's right."

He flung the coat from him. "Never," he said stoutly.

I shrugged. "Okay. If you don't want to be in the swim, I guess it's your business."

I sat down in a chair and pretended to read a book, but out of the corner of my eye I kept watching Petey. He was a torn man. First he looked at the coat with the expression of a waif at a bakery window. Then he turned away and set his jaw resolutely. Then he looked back at the coat, with even more longing in his face. Then he turned away, but with not so much resolution this time. Back and forth his head **swiveled**[②], desire waxing, resolution waning. Finally he didn't turn away at all; he just stood and stared with mad lust at the coat.

---

① canny ['kæni] adj. 精明的，谨慎的；节约的，省俭的；见多识广的，消息灵通的

② swivel ['swɪvəl] v.（使）旋转，（使）转动

“回家度周末。”我草草地给提箱里塞了点东西。

“快看。”周一上午一回来我就找到彼蒂。我飞快地拉开提箱，把眼前这件硕大的毛茸茸的还在散发怪味的东西展示给他。这件浣熊皮大衣还是我父亲在 1925 年开着斯图兹勇士跑车时穿的。

“太好了！”彼蒂崇敬地叹道。他把手插进浣熊皮毛里感受着，随之他的脸也埋了进去，嘴里不断说着，“太好了！”如此重复了一二十遍。

“想要吗？”我问他。

“想啊！”他大喊着把那副油滑的皮毛揽入怀中。紧接着他眼里露出了一丝警惕的神色，“你要从我这换什么呢？”

“你的女朋友。”我直言不讳。

“波莉？”他惊恐地喃喃。“你想要波莉？”

“正是。”

他把大衣撇弃一边。“没门。”他显得很决绝。

我耸耸肩，“好吧。要是你不想跟所谓的潮流的话，我也没什么好勉强你的。”

我搬过一把椅子，假装坐下来看书，可眼角的余光却一直瞟着彼蒂。他陷入了极度的不安中。他先是垂涎地望着这件皮大衣，神情像极了流浪儿驻足于面包店橱窗前的馋样。接着，他扭过头去，下巴坚决地一沉。可没过一会儿，他又回过头去把目光投向那件皮大衣，脸上露出更加渴望的神情。等他再扭过头去时，显然没有刚才那么坚决了。他的头就这么扭过来转过去，愈看愈爱不释手，决心越来越不足。最后他干脆死死地盯住皮大衣，一动不动，眼中噙满贪婪。

"It isn't as though I was in love with Polly," he said thickly. "Or going steady or anything like that."

"That's right," I murmured.

"What's Polly to me, or me to Polly?"

"Not a thing," said I.

"It's just been a casual kick—just a few laughs, that's all."

"Try on the coat," said I.

He complied. The coat bunched high over his ears and dropped all the way down to his shoe tops. He looked like a mound of dead raccoons. "Fits fine," he said happily.

I rose from my chair. "Is it a deal?" I asked, extending my hand.

He **swallowed**①. "It's a deal," he said and shook my hand.

I had my first date with Polly the following evening. This was in the nature of a survey; I wanted to find out just how much work I had to do to get her mind up to the standard I required. I took her first to dinner. "Gee, that was a delish dinner," she said as we left the restaurant. Then I took her to a movie. "Gee, that was a marvy movie," she said as we left the theatre. And then I took her home. "Gee, I had a sensaysh time," she said as she bade me good night.

I went back to my room with a heavy heart. I had gravely underestimated the size of my task. This girl's lack of information was terrifying. Nor would it be enough merely to supply her with information. First she had to be taught to think. This loomed as a project of no small dimensions, and at first I was tempted to give her back to Petey. But then I got to thinking about her abundant physical charms and about the way she entered a room and the way she handled a knife and fork, and I decided to make an effort.

---

① swallow ['swɑlo] v. 吞，咽；吞没，吞并；忍受；食（言）；轻信

“好像我和波莉算不上是在恋爱吧，”他有些含混地说。“也没有确定关系或类似这种。”

“这才对嘛。”我小声附和。

“波莉对我算得了什么？我对波莉又算得了什么？”

“不算什么。”

“只不过是玩玩罢了——在一起寻开心，如此而已。”

“可以试穿了。”我说。

他照做。大衣高高隆起盖住了耳朵，下摆则一直曳到脚面，整个人看上去活像一具浣熊尸体堆在那里。他高兴地说：“挺合适的。”

我从椅子上站起身。“可以成交了吗？”边说边向他伸出了手。

他轻易地就答应了。“成交。”说着握了握我的手。

第二天晚上，我就和波莉第一次约会了。约会的目的其实是考察她，我想先摸清到底我有多少工作要做，才能把她的大脑训练到我的标准。我先带她去吃饭，离开餐馆时她嗲声说：“哇噻，好好吃啊。”然后我又带她去看了场电影，走出影院时她又嗲声说：“哇噻，好好看哪。”再然后我送她回家，临别道晚安时她还是嗲声说：“哇噻，玩得好好呀。”

我心情沉重地回到寝室。我严重地低估了整个任务的艰巨性。这姑娘知识贫乏得不是一点两点，以至于光给她灌输知识也是无济于事的。首先得教会她思考才行。这可绝非易事，浩大工程赫然摆在面前，我都想把这烫手山芋还给彼蒂算了。可转念我又想到她举手投足间的无穷魅力，想到她走进房间时的款款步态，想到她运用刀叉时的娴熟仪态，我还是决定下番功夫。

Love Is a Fallacy (Ⅱ)

爱是谬误（2）

◎ Max Shulman

"Polly," I said to her when I picked her up on our next date, "tonight we are going over to the knoll and talk."

"Oo, terrif," she replied. One thing I will say for this girl: you would go far to find another so agreeable.

We went to the Knoll, the campus **trysting**[①] place, and we sat down under an old oak, and she looked at me expectantly. "What are we going to talk about?" she asked.

"Logic."

She thought this over for a minute and decided she liked it. "Magnif," she said.

"Logic," I said, clearing my throat, "is the science of thinking. Before we can think correctly, we must first learn to recognize the common fallacies of logic. These we will take up tonight."

"Wow-dow!" she cried, clapping her hands delightedly. I **winced**[②], but went bravely on. "First let us examine the fallacy called Dicto Simpliciter."

---

① tryst [trɪst] v. 约会，幽会

② wince [wɪns] v. 畏缩，退缩；面部抽搐，皱眉头

美丽校训励我心

Toronto University: As a tree with the passage of time.

多伦多大学：像大树一样随着时间成长。

“波莉，”当我再次接她约会时，我对她说，“今晚我们去小山那边谈心好吗？”

“喔，太好了。”她应道。得为这姑娘说句公道话：像她这么惟命是从的可不多见。

我们去了小山那儿——校园情侣经常幽会的地方。我们靠着一棵老橡树坐下，她的眼神中满怀期待。“我们要谈些什么呢？”她问。

“逻辑。”

她反应了一阵，觉得自己会喜欢。“不错呀。”她说。

“逻辑，”我清了清嗓子，继续说，“是一门思考的学问。在我们能正确思考之前，必须先学会辨别逻辑上常见的谬误。这就是我们今晚要谈到的内容。”

“哇哦！”她拍手欢呼起来。我不禁一皱眉，但还是鼓起勇气继续。“首先我们来看一下谬误中什么叫绝对判断。”

“当然可以。”她急切地眨巴着眼睛，催促我说下去。

"By all means," she urged, batting her lashes eagerly.

"Dicto Simpliciter means an argument based on an unqualified generalization. For example: Exercise is good. Therefore everybody should exercise."

"I agree," said Polly earnestly. "I mean exercise is wonderful. I mean it builds the body and everything."

"Polly," I said gently, "the argument is a fallacy. Exercise is good is an unqualified generalization. For instance, if you have heart disease, exercise is bad, not good. Many people are ordered by their doctors not to exercise. You must qualify the generalization. You must say exercise is usually good, or exercise is good for most people. Otherwise you have committed a Dicto Simpliciter. Do you see?"

"No," she confessed. "But this is marvy. Do more! Do more!"

"It will be better if you stop tugging at my sleeve," I told her, and when she **desisted**①, I continued. "Next we take up a fallacy called Hasty Generalization. Listen carefully: You can't speak French. Petey Bellows can't speak French. I must therefore conclude that nobody at the University of Minnesota can speak French."

"Really?" said Polly, amazed. "Nobody?" I hid my **exasperation**②. "Polly, it's a fallacy. The generalization is reached too hastily. There are too few instances to support such a conclusion."

"Know any more fallacies?" she asked breathlessly. "This is more fun than dancing even."

I fought off a wave of despair. I was getting nowhere with this girl,

---

① desist [dɪ'sɪst] v. 停止，断念，克制不干

② exasperation [ɪg,zæspə'reʃən] n. 恼怒，激怒；惹人愤怒的事

“绝对判断是指依据无条件泛指得出的论断。举个例子：我们说运动有益。因此人人都应该运动。”

“我同意呀，”波莉一脸诚恳。“我觉得运动很了不起。要我说运动能提高身体素质，强健人体的各个方面。”

“波莉，”我温和地说，“这个论断是有漏洞的。运动有益，这是个无条件的泛指。比如说，假如你患有心脏病，那么运动非但无益，还会有害健康。有不少人遵照医嘱是不能运动的。因此你必须对这个泛指加以限定。你应该说，运动通常是有益的。或者，对大多数人来说运动是有益的。否则你就犯了绝对判断的错误。懂了吗？”

“没懂，”她承认。“但听上去很神。再讲！再讲！”

“你最好别这么拉我的袖子，”我对她说。等她住了手，我继续往下进行。“下面我们来讲讲叫做草率结论的谬误。仔细听好：你不会讲法语。彼蒂·贝勒斯也不会讲法语。因此我推断出明尼苏达大学没人会讲法语。”

“真的吗？”波莉很好奇，“谁都不会？”我压了压火，“波莉，我们在讲谬误。这个推论得出的太草率了，因为能使之成立的例证太少。”

“还有什么好玩的谬误吗？”她因兴奋而呼吸急促，“这可比跳舞有意思多了。”

我极力不让自己陷入沮丧。这姑娘根本不长进，简直是对牛弹琴。不管怎么说，除了坚持下去我别无选择。我看了看表，“我想今晚先到这吧。我送你回家，回去后把刚刚学的回想一下。明晚我们再继续。”

absolutely nowhere. Still, I am nothing if not persistent. I consulted my watch. "I think we'd better call it a night. I'll take you home now, and you go over all the things you've learned. We'll have another session tomorrow night."

Seated under the oak the next evening I said, "Our first fallacy tonight is called Ad Misericordiam." She quivered with delight.

"Listen closely," I said. "A man applies for a job. When the boss asks him what his qualifications are, he replies that he has a wife and six children at home, the wife is a helpless cripple, the children have nothing to eat, no clothes to wear, no shoes on their feet, there are no beds in the house, no coal in the cellar, and winter is coming."

A tear rolled down each of Polly's pink cheeks. "Oh, this is awful, awful," she sobbed."Yes, it's awful," I agreed, "but it's no argument. The man never answered the boss's question about his qualifications. Instead he appealed to the boss's sympathy. He committed the fallacy of Ad Misericordiam. Do you understand?"

"Have you got a handkerchief?" she blubbered.

I handed her a handkerchief and tried to keep from screaming while she wiped her eyes. "Next," I said in a carefully controlled tone, "we will discuss False Analogy. Here is an example: Students should be allowed to look at their textbooks during examinations. After all, surgeons have X-rays to guide them during an operation, lawyers have briefs to guide them during a trial, carpenters have blueprints to guide them when they are building a house. Why, then, shouldn't students be allowed to look at their textbooks during an examination?"

"There now," she said enthusiastically, "is the most marvy idea I've heard in years."

"Polly," I said testily, "the argument is all wrong. Doctors, lawyers, and

次日晚再次坐在橡树下，由我开始，“今晚我们要学的第一个谬误叫做文不对题。”她高兴得一阵颤栗。

“注意听，”我说，“有人想申请工作。老板问他具备什么条件，他回答说家有妻儿。妻子残疾无劳动能力，六个孩子嗷嗷待哺，衣不蔽体打着赤脚。家里穷到没床可睡，没煤取暖，而冬天眼看就要来了。”

眼泪顺着波莉粉红的面颊滑落。“啊，真是太悲惨了，太悲惨了，”她啜泣着。“没错，是挺惨的，”我表示赞同，“但这不是理由。这个人根本没有回答出老板问及的能力问题，而是诉诸同情。他据此犯了文不对题的错误。明白了吗？”

“你带手帕了吗？”她哽咽着问。

我把手帕递给她。看她在那儿只顾抹眼泪，我真忍不住想吼她。“下一个，”我竭力稳住声调，“我们要讨论的是错误类比。看例子：应该允许学生开卷考试。毕竟医生手术时有X光参照，律师出庭时有案宗参照，木匠盖房时有图纸参照，那么，为什么学生考试时就不能有课本参照呢？”

“就这个，”她一下来了兴致，“可算是我这些年来听过的最赞的点子了。”

“波莉，”我开始不耐烦了，“这个论证过程是错的。医生也好，律师还是木匠也罢，他们都不需要通过考试来检验学习效果，只有学生如此。所以，这是完全不同的两种情形，你不能把这两者予以类比。”

“可我还是觉得这主意不错。”波莉说。

carpenters aren't taking a test to see how much they have learned, but students are. The situations are altogether different, and you can't make an analogy between them."

"I still think it's a good idea," said Polly.

"Nuts," I muttered. One more chance, I decided. But just one more. There is a limit to what flesh and blood can bear. "The next fallacy is called Poisoning the Well."

"How cute!" she gurgled.

"Two men are having a debate. The first one gets up and says, 'My opponent is a notorious liar. You can't believe a word that he is going to say.' ... Now, Polly, think. Think hard. What's wrong?" I watched her closely as she knit her creamy brow in concentration. Suddenly a glimmer of intelligence—the first I had seen—came into her eyes. "It's not fair," she said with **indignation**①. "It's not a bit fair. What chance has the second man got if the first man calls him a liar before he even begins talking?"

"Right!" I cried exultantly. "One hundred percent right. It's not fair. The first man has poisoned the well before anybody could drink from it. He has **hamstrung**② his opponent before he could even start ... Polly, I'm proud of you."

"Pshaws," she murmured, blushing with pleasure.

"You see, my dear, these things aren't so hard. All you have to do is concentrate. Think—examine—evaluate. Come now, let's review everything we have learned."

"Fire away," she said with an airy wave of her hand.

Heartened by the knowledge that Polly was not altogether a cretin, I began

---

① indignation [ˌɪndɪɡ'neʃən] n. 愤怒，愤慨，义愤

② hamstring ['hæmˌstrɪŋ] v. 割断……的腘腱，使瘸腿；使无能为力，削弱……的活动能力

“神经病。”我咕哝着。再试一个，我不死心。就最后一个。常人的忍耐终究是有限度的。“下一个谬误叫井下投毒。”

“好有趣的说法！”她咯咯笑。

“两个人在争辩。第一个先站起身说，‘我的对手是个声名狼藉的骗子，他所说的每一句话都不可信。’……现在，波莉，你想想看，好好想想，这话里有什么问题？”我目不转睛地看着她，只见她细密如脂的双眉在极度思索中凝成一团。突然间，她眼中似灵光乍现，这可是我第一次见她这样。“这不公平，”她很气愤。“一点都不公平。第二个人还没等开口就被第一个人说成了骗子，那他还怎么为自己辩护啊？”

“太对了！”我大喜过望地喊了出来。“百分之百正确。就是不公平。第一个人先于井中下了毒，以致其他人都无法喝到井水。他还不待对手开口就先行中伤了他……波莉，我真为你骄傲。”

“哪有。”她小声说，喜得面庞都红了。

“亲爱的，看到了吧，这些问题并没有那么难。你要做的就是用心。思考——审视——评判，如此三步。来，我们把所学过的东西再一起复习一遍。”

“开始吧。”她边说边快活地晃了晃手臂。

看到波莉还不至于那么冥顽不灵，我也来劲了，领着她开始了漫长而又耐心的复习过程。一遍又一遍地，我反复列举例子，指出漏洞，不知疲

a long, patient review of all I had told her. Over and over and over again I cited instances, pointed out flaws, kept hammering away without letup. It was like digging a tunnel. Five grueling nights with this took, but it was worth it. I had made a logician out of Polly; I had taught her to think. My job was done. She was worthy of me, at last. It must not be thought that I was without love for this girl. Quite the contrary. Just as Pygmalion loved the perfect woman he had fashioned, so I loved mine. I decided to acquaint her with my feelings at our very next meeting. The time had come to change our relationship from academic to romantic.

"Polly," I said when next we sat beneath our oak, "tonight we will not discuss fallacies."

"Aw, gee," she said, disappointed. "My dear," I said, favoring her with a smile, "we have now spent five evenings together. We have gotten along splendidly. It is clear that we are well matched."

"Hasty Generalization," said Polly brightly. "I beg your pardon," said I. "Hasty Generalization," she repeated. "How can you say that we are well matched on the basis of only five dates?" I chuckled with amusement. The dear child had learned her lessons well. "My dear," I said, patting her hand in a tolerant manner, "five dates is plenty. After all, you don't have to eat a whole cake to know that it's good."

"False Analogy," said Polly promptly. "I'm not a cake. I'm a girl." I chuckled with somewhat less amusement. The dear child had learned her lessons perhaps too well. I decided to change tactics. Obviously the best approach was a simple, strong, direct declaration of love. I paused for a moment while my massive brain chose the proper word. Then I began: "Polly, I love you. You are the whole world to me, the moon and the stars and the constellations of outer

倦地灌输下去。这个过程就好似在挖一条隧道。整整辛苦了五个晚上，努力总算没有白费。我终于将波莉打造成了逻辑学家，我教会了她如何思考。大功告成，她终于配得上我了。不要以为我对这姑娘毫无感情，恰恰相反。正如皮格马利翁珍爱他一手塑造的完美女神一样，我也非常爱我的波莉。我决定下次见面时向她告白，是时候把我们的关系由师生转化为男女之情了。

“波莉，”当我们再次坐在橡树下时，我说，“今晚我们不需要讨论谬误了。”

“唔，不好玩，”她显得很失望。“亲爱的，”我一脸笑意地讨好她，“我们已经一起度过了五个美妙的夜晚，相处十分融洽。显然我们两个很相配。”

“草率结论，”波莉伶俐地回应。“再说一遍，”我有点懵。“草率结论，”她重复给我。“你怎能仅凭短短的五次约会就断定我们很相配呢？”我饶有兴致地暗自发笑。我的可人儿功课学得可真不错。“亲爱的，”我带着纵容之意拍拍她的手，“五次约会就不少了呀。毕竟你也不需要吃下整个蛋糕就可以尝出味道的好坏来啊。”

“错误类比，”波莉反应敏捷。“我可不是蛋糕，我是女孩子。”这回我笑得有点勉强。我的可人儿功课怕是学得太好了。我决定改变策略。显然，最好的办法莫过于简单直接地深情向她示爱。我沉吟了片刻，用我发达的大脑检索着最恰切的字眼。然后我咏叹道：“波莉，我爱你。你就是我的全世界，是月亮，是星辰，是宇宙的全部星宿。请你，我亲爱的，许给我这

space. Please, my darling, say that you will go steady with me, for if you will not, life will be meaningless. I will languish. I will refuse my meals. I will wander the face of the earth, a shambling, hollow-eyed hulk." There, I thought, folding my arms, that ought to do it.

"Ad Misericordiam," said Polly. I ground my teeth. I was not Pygmalion; I was Frankenstein, and my monster had me by the throat. Frantically I fought back the tide of panic surging through me; at all costs I had to keep cool. "Polly," I croaked, "you mustn't take all these things so literally. I mean this is just classroom stuff. You know that the things you learn in school don't have anything to do with life."

"Dicto Simpliciter," she said, wagging her finger at me playfully. That did it. I leaped to my feet, bellowing like a bull. "Will you or will you not go steady with me?"

"I will not," she replied.

"Why not?" I demanded.

"Because this afternoon I promised Petey Bellows that I would go steady with him." I reeled back, overcome with the **infamy**① of it. After he promised, after he made a deal, after he shook my hand! "The rat!" I shrieked, kicking up great chunks of turf. "You can't go with him, Polly. He's a liar. He's a cheat. He's a rat."

"Poisoning the Well ," said Polly, "and stop shouting. I think shouting must be a fallacy too."

With an immense effort of will, I **modulated**② my voice. "All right," I said. "You're a logician. Let's look at this thing logically. How could you choose Petey

---

① infamy ['ɪnfəmi] n. 臭名，声名狼藉；恶行，丑事

② modulate ['mɑdʒəˌlet] v. 调节，调整；转调，变调

一生。如果你拒绝了我，我的生命将失去意义。我将从此萎靡下去，不思茶饭，如一具空壳游荡世间，步履蹒跚，两眼深陷。”话已至此，我含情脉脉地张着双臂，心想，这下一定可以打动她。

“文不对题。”波莉不为所动。我牙齿磨得嘎吱响。我哪里是皮格马利翁，我分明是弗兰肯斯坦，被我的怪兽扼住了喉咙。我拼命控制住内心泛起的恐慌。无论如何，我都要保持冷静。“波莉，”我声音嘶哑，“不要死板地搬弄这些知识。我是说，这些在课堂上运用一下就够了。你知道，学校里学来的东西与现实并不搭界。”

“绝对判断。”她说道，还戏弄地朝我摇了摇手指。这下我彻底火了。我气得跳脚，公牛般咆哮。“你到底要不要跟我在一起？”

“不要。”她回答。

“为什么不？”我追问。

“因为今天下午我答应了彼蒂·贝勒斯要和他在一起。”我被彼蒂的无耻之举怔住，不由得倒退了几步。这厮不是一脸诚恳地许诺了么，不是说好跟我做交易的么，不是还假惺惺地握了我的手么！“卑鄙的家伙！”我一声尖叫，把脚下的一大块草皮踢了起来。“你不能跟他在一起，波莉。他撒谎，他骗人，他可耻。”

“井下投毒，”波莉接过话茬，“别嚷嚷了。我想大声叫嚷也算是一种谬误吧。”

我以极大的意志力缓和住语气。“好吧，”我认输。“现在你是逻辑学家。那就让我们用逻辑来分析一下这件事。你怎么会选择彼蒂·贝勒斯而不选择我呢？看看我——有才华，有学识，有前途。再看看彼蒂——易冲

Bellows over me? Look at me—a brilliant student, a tremendous intellectual, a man with an assured future. Look at Petey—a knothead, a jitterbug, a guy who'll never know where his next meal is coming from. Can you give me one logical reason why you should go steady with Petey Bellows?"

"I certainly can," declared Polly. "He's got a raccoon coat."

动，易紧张，就是个连明天都不晓得在哪的家伙。你能给我个合乎逻辑的理由吗，为什么要跟彼蒂·贝勒斯在一起？”

“当然可以，”波莉毫不示弱。“他有浣熊皮大衣。”

Deck the Halls

装点圣诞

◎ Melanie Fester

Christmas in my house was always a major event. My mom insisted that we play Christmas music and only Christmas music—all the time and starting two weeks before the "big day". We'd bake Santa-shaped cookies and give them to our friends and neighbors. Every year, my sister and I decorated the house with porcelain figurines that had been in the family for **eons**[①]. Each year we'd track down the perfect tree at the local "U-Cut" Christmas-tree farm.

Of course, I'll admit that there were times when the mere thought of spending yet another Saturday listening to Bing and Mom **crooning**[②] "White Christmas" made me want to stuff a stocking down any songster's merry little throat. And the prospect of my annual fight with my sister over the ideal shape of a Douglas fir was about as appealing as, say, running into Steve Urkel under the mistletoe.

Then I went to college. Sure, there was no **curfew**[③], no obligatory family dinners; but when December rolled around, there was also no baking, decorating

---

① eon ['iən] n. 极漫长的时期，万古，千万年

② croon [krun] v. 低声哼唱，轻吟；悲叹，呻吟

③ curfew ['kə:fju] n. 宵禁，宵禁令，宵禁时间

美丽校训励我心

University of Sydney: The stars change, the mind the same.

悉尼大学：斗转星移，我心永恒。

圣诞对我们家来说一直都是个重大活动。距离这个“大日子”还有两周开始，妈妈就会让我们天天播放圣诞音乐，并且只许放圣诞音乐。我们会烘焙出圣诞老人形状的饼干，分发给我们的朋友和邻居。每一年，姐姐和我都会翻出那些老家底似的陶瓷小雕像来装饰房间。年年我们都要到当地的“原生态”圣诞树农场，去挑选一棵最好的圣诞树。

当然，我得承认，有时候光是想想我在周末又要听着妈妈跟随平·克劳斯贝一起深情合唱《白色圣诞》，我就恨不得拿圣诞袜套堵住这些歌手那轻快的小嗓。而每年我和姐姐都会为了冷杉的理想形状打得不可开交，这场好戏的看头要我说来，不亚于在槲寄生下撞见了斯蒂夫·厄克尔。

然后我就上了大学。这下肯定没有宵禁一说了，也没有一家人聚餐的义务了；可是当 12 月又临近之时，曾经的烘培时光、装饰活动，乃至圣诞音乐也都随着消失不见了。剩下的只有考前的恐慌，以及凌晨 3 点还在狂

or music. Just the exam panic and 3:00 A.M. diet soda **binges**①. By December 13, with ten more anxiety-filled days to go before my last final, I was totally depressed and desperately homesick. I decided to take action.

"This stinks," I declared to my equally stressed-out roommate. "Put down your highlighter pen. I need a little Christmas, right this very minute. Carols at the window, candles on the spinet!" It was bad. I was leaking **sappy**② Christmas tunes from home, and I knew I had to do something about it—quick! Luckily, my roommate was feeling the same way. We both tossed our books aside and prepared to outdo Macy's with our version of Christmas cheer.

In a Martha Stewart-like frenzy, we fashioned red and green construction paper into signs that read "MERRY XMAS" and taped them to our walls. Then we cut snowflake **wannabes**③ from typing paper and made our own winter wonderland. We microwaved popcorn, strung some of it, ate most of it, and then hung the strings artfully around the room.

Finally, we stepped back to examine our work. Something was missing. Andy Williams singing "Joy to the World"? Antler headbands? No, duh—lights! So we grabbed a cab to the nearest discount store and bought miles of multicolored bulbs.

Back in our room, we went through three rolls of duct tape trying to get the look we so desperately craved. Around the door, veering **erratically**④ across the ceiling and up the window, we fashioned an impressionistic Christmas-tree shape. When we plugged the lights in, it was a sight to behold. I popped a Christmas tape that my mom had sent me into the tape deck, and the moment was

---

① binge [bɪndʒ] n. 狂欢作乐，狂饮；无节制的狂热行动；社交集会

② sappy ['sapi] adj. 树汁多的；精力充沛的；多愁善感的

③ wannabe ['wɑnə,bi] n. 效仿者

④ erratically [ɪ'rætɪkli] adv. 不规则地，不定地；古怪地，反常地

饮低糖苏打水提神醒脑。捱到 12 月 13 日，距离期末考试还有十来天，想想自己还要在焦虑中度过，我彻底郁闷了，并且极度想家。我决定采取措施。

"真是糟透了，"我向同样快要被压力逼疯的室友们抱怨，"放下你们手中的记号笔。我需要点圣诞的感觉，一刻都等不及了。窗户里飘出颂歌，琴台上燃着蜡烛！"这可不好，我竟多愁善感地在哼家中的圣诞曲了。我知道我得为此做点什么——要快！好在我的室友们也都有着同样的情绪。我们不约而同地把书抛向一边，开始着手筹备我们自己的圣诞庆祝活动，大有赶超梅西百货之势呢。

在一阵玛莎·斯图尔特般的狂潮中，我们用红色和绿色的美术纸制作出了"圣诞快乐"的字样，粘贴在墙上。我们又用打印纸裁出雪花的形状，布置出我们的冰雪仙境。我们还用微波加热出爆米花，吃掉了大部分，留下一小部分巧妙地一串串穿起来，悬挂在房间里。

最后，我们退远些看了看效果，好像缺了点什么。少了安迪·威廉姆斯演唱的《普世欢腾》？少了鹿角头饰？哦，不——是少了彩灯！于是我们拦下一辆的士，赶往最近的打折卖场，买下了好几米长的彩灯泡。

回到寝室，急于营造出想要的效果，我们用光了三卷密封胶带。门的四周环了一圈，向顶棚不规则地铺过去，又搭在窗子上，绕出一个印象派的圣诞树形状。当我们通上电，灯泡亮起来时，眼前的景象令我们都看呆了。我把妈妈寄给我的磁带倏地塞进收音机里，圣诞音乐响起来，这一时刻终于圆满了。

complete.

To further foster the feeling of Christmas, I insisted that the group of girls on my floor do a secret Santa gift exchange. Everybody drew a name out of a hat and bought that person a gift. Then we all got together, opened our presents and tried to guess who our secret Santa was. Sitting there in a sea of shower gels, posters of cute guys and Lifesaver's Sweet Storybooks, I started choking up. It was at that moment I realized how special, wonderful and beautiful my mom had made this holiday for all of us in our family. It was a part of me, even if I was locked in a dorm with a bunch of girls cramming for exams, I had to have it.

Sure, it was Christmas college-style with Rice Krispy treats instead of rice pudding, and Pearl Jam instead of the Hallelujah Chorus; but we were stuck at school, and we got to create our own traditions. I'm a senior now, and we still do the secret Santa thing. My roommate and I have also lugged boxes of ornaments and hauled nasty-looking fake Christmas trees around from dorms to two apartments, but as long as I live, I will never forget our first heartfelt, makeshift college Christmas.

为了更好地加深圣诞气氛，我提议让我们这一层的女孩相互间秘密交换圣诞礼物。我们把每个人的名字做成纸条放在帽子里，大家抽到谁就给谁准备一份礼物。然后我们都聚到一起，拆开各自的礼物，猜猜自己的这位神秘圣诞老人是谁。坐拥着一大堆的沐浴露、帅哥海报以及“救生圈”故事书装薄荷糖，我禁不住抽噎起来。那一刻我突然意识到，妈妈精心为我们这一家人布置出的圣诞节日是多么特别，多么精彩，多么美妙。它已经成为我无法割舍的一部分，哪怕是我被关在寝室和一屋女孩为考试忙得昏天暗地之际，我还是需要这个节日陪伴我。

当然，我们的这个圣诞是象牙塔风格的，米通充当了米饭布丁，Pearl Jam 乐队替代了哈利路亚大合唱；然而，我们正被困在学校里，只能自己这样变通传统。如今我已经读大四了，我们仍在庆祝圣诞交换神秘礼物。哪怕是一再地更换住处，我和室友还是会不怕费力地拖拽上满盒子的装饰品和难看的塑料圣诞树，在寝室和两处公寓楼间辗转。恐怕在这一生中，我永远都不会忘记最初在学校过的那个临时拼凑但却情真意切的圣诞节。

My Graduation Trip
毕业旅行

© Shogo Kanayama

At the end of that year, it snowed even in Sakai: a small town in Osaka where snow has seldom lain, most likely, because of global warming. I looked out of the window, when fine snow was falling silently under a **bleak**① overcast sky. Before long, the snow turned to large snowflakes and began fluttering down ceaselessly. Everything in my temple-yard became white with snow in an instant, and silence settled over the surroundings.

The snow landscape reminds me of my school days. I will never forget the simplicity and the sentiment I had on my solitary trip to the northern region of Japan before graduating from university. It was snowing lightly on a February night when I finished writing my graduation thesis. I packed up my few belongings and left my rooming house for Ueno Station to take a night train bound for Sendai, holding a one-week discount excursion ticket tightly in my hand. In those days, it was popular for poor students to go youth-hostelling with a student discount. I could get on and off over and over again at any station for a five-thousand-yen ticket, by express but with an unreserved seat, and to lodge for five hundred yen per night. The price included two meals as well. Hunger is the best sauce; that was no time to be picky about the food. I thought that trip might

① bleak [blik] adj. 无遮蔽的，荒凉的，阴冷的；惨淡的；冷酷的

美丽校训励我心

University of Auckland: By natural ability and hard work.

奥克兰大学：天赋辅以勤奋。

那一年岁暮，连堺市也下起了雪：这个位于大阪府的小城很少飘雪，很可能是全球变暖的效应吧。我向窗外望去，无声的细雪从布满阴霾的天空簌簌落下。没多久，就变成了大片的雪花，漫天不停地纷纷扬扬。我落脚的这座寺庙很快被白雪覆盖了，草木沙石披上了银装，四周一片阒寂。

眼前的雪景令我忆起我的学生时代。我无法忘怀大学临毕业前的那次旅行，我一个人怀着单纯的心意及无名的惆怅去往日本北部。2月的夜晚，当我秉笔做完毕业论文之际，外面正有雪飘飘洒洒。我收拾起本不多的个人物品，离开公寓，前往上野车站搭乘去仙台的夜车，彼时手里正紧紧攥着一周使用期的折扣优待票。那时候，穷学生普遍会选择享受学生优惠的青年旅馆入住。我可以花五千日元买张通票，一路走走停停。途中可以选择特快，只是座位不能预留。住宿每晚只消五百日元，提供两餐。饥饿感可谓最好的佐料，让人没时间对食物挑挑拣拣。我思量着这该是我最后一

be the last chance for me to use the student discount. Some friends from the snowy district said that it was a ridiculous idea to make a trip on such cold days simply because I wanted to see snow, not to ski. But no matter what anybody said, I just wanted to see a snow landscape as the last memory of my school days; I had had a strong yearning for the life in a region with heavy snowfalls. Actually, I had no interest in skiing, or rather I could not afford to, I should say. I was living on a tight budget and I had no money to spare. Such an expensive sport was simply beyond my means. I lived on a monthly allowance and a part-time job, but the most part of it usually ended up being spent on drinking. I used to go on a **spree**① with my friends, then finally I got fed up with it. I wanted to outgrow my playful but **frivolous**② mood in those college days. So I got the idea of going on a trip in an attempt to make a clean break from my **flippant**③ days.

Despite the fact that it was almost eleven, Ueno Station, one of the terminal stations for the Tohoku region, was congested with passengers carrying large packages in their hands or on their shoulders. The bell rang loudly each time trains arrived and departed, and just hearing the repeated announcements over the station PA system got on my nerves. Crusted snow was stuck to the window frames of the train which had just arrived from Aomori, giving a **shudder**④ and grinding to a halt. The paint was off in places and rust had eaten deeply into the metal parts of the old car. Many people poured out of the cars with exhausted looks on their faces. I sat on a bench and savoured a can of beer. That was what I had wanted, I would soon be a man in a carefree solitary trip. I was alone in the buzz of conversation watching those who came and went. Though it was

---

① spree [spri] n. 嬉戏，欢闹；狂欢作乐；无节制的狂热行为

② frivolous ['frɪvələs] adj. 轻薄的，轻浮的；琐屑的，不重要的

③ flippant ['flɪpənt] adj. 轻率的，无礼的，轻浮的

④ shudder ['ʃʌdɚ] n. 突然震动；战栗，打颤

次享受这优待了。我那些在冰天雪地中生活的朋友都不大理解我会在这样寒冷的天气里想要去往北部，目的却不是滑雪，只是赏景。但不管别人怎么说，我一度很向往到大雪覆盖的地方生活，因此我执意要把这雪国之姿融入学生时代的最后记忆；事实上，我对滑雪并不作兴，或者说是我负担不起，倒更切实。我的生活节衣缩食，并无闲钱。这样一种花费不菲的运动显然超出了我的经济能力。我靠每月的补贴和做兼职过活，但这些钱大部分都用来买醉了。我曾放纵自己与朋友们狂欢畅饮，但最终我还是厌倦了这个样子的我。我想摆脱大学以来这种玩世不恭、不务正业的心境。因此我决定拿起行囊漂泊一次，让我的精神与轻浮的过去彻底决裂。

即便已经夜里 11 点了，作为东北地区交通枢纽的上野车站还是人头攒动，满是手提或肩扛大包的旅客。每当有火车进出站台，就会有尖锐的铃声响起。广播里不断重复播报着列车信息，听起来颇使人烦。由青森开来的夜车咣当一震，咔嚓嚓停了下来。冻住的积雪挂在窗框上，车身的漆面已经有些斑驳了，铁皮的厢体也被侵蚀得锈迹斑斑。好多人一脸疲惫地涌出车厢。我坐在长椅上，呷着啤酒。这种感觉正是我想要的，不久我就要独自一人踏上闲适的旅程。我游离于嘈杂的环境音外，看着那些人来来往往。尽管已近午夜时分，可车站外依旧灯火通明，根本寻不到人们的一丝

around midnight, I could not even see their shades in the brightly lit station yard. A constant noise, brilliant **fluorescent**[1] lights and the smell of diesel fumes in the air.

"Unless I leave this hustle and bustle of the city, there is no way to get rid of my fatigue," I mumbled, bidding farewell in my mind to the carefree days of my youth, drinking a toast to myself with the rest of the beer.

① fluorescent [flʊəˈrɛsənt] adj. 荧光的；发亮的，强反光的；容光焕发的

影子。空间里流荡着持续不断的噪音，明亮泛白的灯光，以及挥之不去的燃油气味。

“除非离开这熙熙攘攘的城市，否则我没法赶走这副疲惫。”我喃喃自语，在心里阔别了那些肆无忌惮的青春，为自己举杯祝觞，喝光了余下的啤酒。

Ode to Schoollife

校园生活颂歌

◎ Moz Rauf

In my dreams, sometimes
Your eyes turn, black and white
And we stare the black-board together
Till the speeding chalk, screams a dirty noise
And whenever I look outside the corner window of the classroom
The sun would always, quietly smile
Down that empty hockey field
Where, we would make smoke-rings
As wild as my beloved's raven eyes!

Now you know how I played hide and seek
With my killing numerical plight
Whenever the mathematics teacher cried
Matrixes, my boys, are a way of life!

Now that the numbers are written all over my face
And the smoke-rings have flown to a distant space
I know how well the matrixes rhyme
And why not to wake up in the middle of a dream!

在我的梦中，有时候

透过你的眼孔，一切都变成黑白

我们一起注视着黑板

直到飞速挥动的粉笔，划出尖厉刺耳的噪音

每当我从教室窗户的一角向外望去

太阳总是悬在当空，静静照耀

日光倾泻在空荡荡的曲棍球场

在那，我们吐着烟圈

狂野得好似恋人乌黑的眼睛！

现在你知道我如何

同我那要命的数字难题躲猫猫

每当数学老师站在那声嘶力竭

矩阵，我的孩子们，是人生之路！

既然这些数字已全然写在我的脸上

那些烟圈也飘向了远方

我才明白这些矩阵是多么顺口

而又是为什么不要从未完的梦中醒来！

Wherever you go,

no matter what the weather,

always bring your own sunshine.

不论去向何方，

不管境遇如何，

时刻有份阳光心情。